Hiking Waterfalls in Washington

Hiking Waterfalls in Washington

A Guide to the State's Best Waterfall Hikes

Roddy Scheer with Adam Sawyer

FALCONGUIDES

GUILFORD, CONNECTICUT
HELENA, MONTANA

An imprint of Rowman & Littlefield
Falcon, FalconGuides, and Outfit Your Mind are registered trademarks of Rowman & Littlefield.

Distributed by NATIONAL BOOK NETWORK

Maps by Roberta Stockwell © Rowman & Littlefield

British Library Cataloguing-in-Publication Information Available

Library of Congress Cataloging-in-Publication Data
Scheer, Roddy.
   Hiking waterfalls in Washington : a guide to the state's best waterfall hikes / Roddy Scheer with Adam Sawyer.
      pages cm
   Includes index.
   ISBN 978-0-7627-8728-9 (pbk.) — ISBN 978-1-4930-1446-0 (e-book) 1.   Hiking—Washington—Guidebooks. 2. Waterfalls—Washington—Guidebooks. 3. Washington—Guidebooks. I. Sawyer, Adam, 1974- II. Title.
   GV199.42.W17S37 2015
   796.5109797—dc23
                                        2015003365

∞™ The paper used in this publication meets the minimum requirements of American National Standard for Information Sciences—Permanence of Paper for Printed Library Materials, ANSI/NISO Z39.48-1992.

Contents

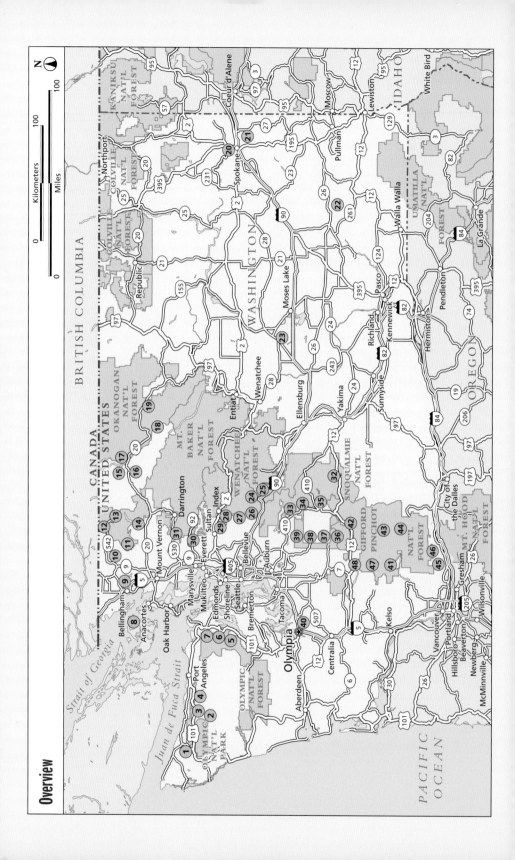

Overview

Acknowledgments

Putting together this book has truly been a labor of love, requiring miles and miles in the family van and hours and hours away from home. That said, I couldn't have done it without the loving support and utter patience of my wife, Alex, and kids, Eliza and Max. And special thanks to my parents, Ruth and Ken, who have always set such a good example for me and let me blaze my own trails.

I am indebted to (and a little furious at) Allen Cox, my editor at *Northwest Travel* magazine, for referring this wonderful bear of a project to me. Thanks to John Burbidge, my original FalconGuides editor on the project, for getting my feet wet, so to speak, and to Katie Benoit, who took the book on midstream and expertly guided it to completion.

Bryan Swan's Northwest Waterfall Survey, part of the larger World Waterfall Database, has proven an invaluable resource in researching which of Washington's thousands of named cascades to include in this book. Swan keeps busy 9-to-5 as a technology professional, but spends the rest of his time exploring waterfalls, documenting what he finds, and adding new information to the World Waterfall Database.

Likewise, Aaron's Waterfall World, a website featuring descriptions and pictures of waterfalls in northwest Washington State by Aaron Young, has been a great aid in helping me sort through which of the hundreds of named waterfalls around Bellingham and the North Cascades to cover.

Another great source of data and description has been the Washington Trails Association (WTA) website, which is chock-full of thousands of hiking trail descriptions from the Pacific coast of the Olympic Peninsula to the Idaho border. This nonprofit has been operating since 1966 maintaining hiking trails and working to protect wild lands, mostly with volunteer labor, and correctly considers itself the "voice" for hikers in Washington State.

As for gear, I will be forever indebted to Volkswagen for making the Eurovan, and wish they would bring back a new small camper so I could finally upgrade. My 2003 pop-top edition has taken me into many remote areas and provided a comfortable home on wheels and wilderness charging station in the field. For photography, I have relied on Nikon gear ever since my dad shipped me his then 24-year-old Nikon FM body and a couple of prime lenses before I embarked on my first trip to Alaska in 2001. Taking good pictures with that old-school manual film camera and manual-focus lenses taught me all I needed to know about photography. That gear, and lots more (especially now that we are into the digital age), has helped me document my travels, wild and otherwise, ever since.

Most of all, I'd like to acknowledge and thank you, the reader, for your interest in waterfalls, hiking, and wild, natural places—and for buying this guidebook, which was prepared with so much sweat and joy. Enjoy it, and see you out on the trail!

—Roddy

Introduction

While it's hard to say which US state has the most waterfalls, Washington—dominated as it is by glaciated peaks, rushing rivers, and lots and lots of precipitation—is definitely near the top of the list. Wherever you might ramble throughout the state, from the verdant rain forests of the Olympic Peninsula to the snowy peaks of the Cascade range (named by Lewis and Clark when they saw the mountains looming above a "cascade" in the Columbia River) to the high, dry deserts of Eastern Washington, waterfalls are indeed everywhere.

Meanwhile, three national parks, five sprawling national forests, one national volcanic monument, and more than one hundred state parks, not to mention thousands of regional and municipal parklands, make Washington a mecca for nature lovers and outdoors enthusiasts. In fact, almost 42 percent of the state's total land mass—or some 17.8 million acres—is in the public trust in one form or another. So chances are wherever you live or visit in Washington, there is good hike nearby, and it might well involve visiting a waterfall.

The purpose of this book is to make it easier to find and access some of the best waterfalls in the state. The knowledge on the topic I have accumulated over 15 years of exploring the state as a travel writer and outdoor photographer is now in your hands. Now that you've invested in the book, you owe it yourself to stuff it into a backpack and hit the trail. I can just picture you now, sitting at the base of a beautiful waterfall in a forest hollow deep in the Cascades, breathing in mood-boosting negative ions and eating the best-tasting sandwich you've ever made yourself. Picturing you there is why I wrote this book, so make sure to get up and out and ensure my vision becomes a reality.

Weather

While Seattle is famous around the world for its drizzly winters, the weather in Washington State isn't all bad. For starters, it varies greatly depending on which side of the Cascade mountain range you happen to be on. Seattle, which is on Puget Sound on the western side of the mountains, gets about 38 inches of rain annually, while Spokane in Eastern Washington gets less than half that much rain throughout the year.

In general, the best time to visit Washington if waterfall hiking is a goal would be spring and early summer, when warming temperatures trigger snowmelt in the mountains that in turn feeds the rivers and their waterfalls below. On the west side of the Cascades (including all the regions covered in this book except for Eastern Washington), high temperatures in July typically hit 75–80 degrees Fahrenheit during the day with lows in the mid-50s at night—with little if any rain! In fact, the regional climate shifts from a wintertime wet pattern into a seasonal drought every summer, making the Pacific Northwest a great place to be anytime from early July through mid-September. On the flip side, Decembers can be cold and wet: Average daytime highs top out in the mid-40s and lows 10 degrees cooler, and more than 5 inches of rain spreads itself out across 17 of the 31 days of the month on average.

Meanwhile, east of the Cascades, far from the reach of the marine layer over the North Pacific that moderates temperatures in Seattle and environs, summers are hotter and winters are colder. In Spokane, 200 miles east of Seattle on the high and dry Columbia River plateau, midsummer temperatures typically reach into the mid-80s or hotter with nighttime lows down in the mid-50s. Six months later the average highs only hit 32 degrees Fahrenheit, with nighttime lows another 10 degrees cooler. Brrrrr indeed!

Flora and Fauna

Like the weather, the flora and fauna of Washington vary depending on which side of the Cascade range you are on. West-side forests are dominated by Douglas firs and western red cedars—some of which top out above 200 feet tall and have been alive since before Columbus discovered the New World—not to mention Sitka spruces, western hemlocks, red alders and vine maples, among other iconic trees of the region. On the east side of the mountains, ponderosa pines, Engelmann spruces, western larches, and a cadre of other trees that prefer drier soils and ambient conditions thrive. And as you get farther east, desert plants like sagebrush and rabbitbrush can make off-trail travel a prickly affair.

In terms of wildlife, deer, elk, black bear, coyote, cougar, raccoon, and various rodents are dispersed in varying numbers statewide. The old-growth forests of the Olympic Peninsula are home to the spotted owl, that controversial symbol of the environmental movement in the 1990s as the federal government shut down access to millions of acres of timberland to protect the bird from extinction. A small population of grizzly (brown) bears is reputed to live in the northern reaches of the North Cascades but sightings have been few and far between. East of the Cascades, hikers should be careful where they step, as rattlesnakes have been known to pop out of the shadows from under a rock or bush when you least expect it. Coyotes and bighorn sheep also play an important role in the ecosystems of Eastern Washington. As always, when you encounter wild animals, give them plenty of space so they don't feel threatened or boxed in and can get away easily. Remember, they are probably more scared of you than you are of them, so enjoy seeing them and let them move along.

Wilderness Restrictions/Regulations

Like many western states, Washington has an embarrassment of riches when it comes to public lands, but navigating which passes are needed where remains an issue for those trying to access the outdoors. The vast majority of the waterfalls covered in this book are on public land, but different jurisdictions have different rules regarding where and when you can park a car and access hiking trails and backcountry campsites. Below is an overview of what you need to know by agency:

Map Legend

Municipal

≡⬡5⬡≡ Interstate Highway

≡(2)≡ US Highway

≡(113)≡ State Road

≡[2530]≡ Forest/Local Road

==== Gravel Road

==== Unpaved Road

•——• Power Line

+—+—+ Railroad

—··—·· State Boundary

Trails

-------- Featured Trail

------- Trail

Water Features

Body of Water

River/Creek

Intermittent Stream

Waterfall

Spring

Glacier

Symbols

≍ Bridge

■ Building/Point of Interest

▲ Campground

▲ Campsite

🅿 Parking

≍ Pass

▲ Peak/Elevation

🄰 Picnic Area/Day-Use Park

🄵 Ranger Station

🄺 Scenic View

🎿 Ski Area

🏛 Tower

○ Town

(20) Trailhead

❓ Visitor/Information Center

Land Management

National Park/Forest

National Recreation/Scenic Area

Ski Area

State/County Park

Olympic Peninsula and Islands

The Olympic Peninsula in the northwest corner of the continental United States, home to high glacial peaks, wild free-flowing rivers, and lush temperate rain forests, is one of the most beautiful parts of Washington State. The rough-and-tumble topography of the region is the result of ancient tectonic forces—think continental plates bumping up against each other and causing uplift—and then, a little more recently, the glaciation of the last ice age some 10,000 years ago. Unlike the Cascades, the Olympic range is not of volcanic origin, and as a result is composed primarily of sandstone and basalt, not granite. This unique

The Olympic Peninsula is famous for its lush, green temperate rain forest among other natural charms.

geological composition is part of what gives the Olympics their wild, impenetrable character and sets the region apart from other wild and woolly parts of Washington State.

Despite the difficult terrain, humans may have inhabited the Olympic Peninsula for longer than anywhere else in what is today considered the continental United States. Stone tools excavated there have been dated back some 7,600 years, following the end of the last ice age and early humans' journey over the Bering Strait into North America. Indeed, the Native coastal Salish tribes who called the region home for thousands of years prior to white settlement lived well off abundant natural resources, including wild game and seafood and a wide range of edible native plants. According to Indian lore, Olympic Peninsula rivers were so clogged with salmon during the summer runs that you didn't need a footbridge to cross over them.

While white settlement of the Northwest in the mid-1800s brought the first roads and trails to the region, the Olympics remained the last frontier for many more years. In 1890 a five-man media expedition looking to explore and survey the peninsula finally made it through the Olympics' tangled and steep interior and out to the coast after a 6-month ordeal during one of the coldest and snowiest winters in memory. Adventurers have been following in their footsteps and blazing their own new trails ever since. But don't think for a second that Washington's wildest region is tamed in any way. There might not be a more remote spot in the Lower 48 than in the middle of the temperate rain forest of "Valley of 10,000 Waterfalls" under the shadow of 9,573-foot Mt. Olympus in the middle of the Olympic Peninsula.

Camping and Accommodations

Falls View Campground, Quilcene, WA: This Olympic National Forest campground has thirty sites suitable for tents or RVs ($10/night) spread across two loops and provides quick access to lots of hikes—the overlook of Falls View Falls is a few feet away from the campsites—as well as the waterfront of nearby Quilcene Bay and its oyster and clam bed. From Quilcene, WA, drive 3.5 miles south on US 101 to the Falls View Campground entrance on the west side of the road. Open May through September, weather permitting. www.fs.usda.gov/recarea/olympic/recarea/?recid=47829. GPS: N47 47.373'/W122 55.712'

Lake Crescent Lodge, Olympic National Park, WA: Built in 1916, this classic lodge and resort on the southern shore of cerulean Lake Crescent offers up fifty-two guestrooms in eleven different room/cabin configurations ($119–$282/night)—not to mention a great restaurant and canoe, rowboat, kayak, and paddleboard rentals. Even if you're not staying there, the lodge's lobby, with its big stone fireplace and antique furniture, is an inviting place to stop for a drink or snack before or after a hike to nearby Marymere Falls. The lodge is only open May through January, but some of the historic Roosevelt Cabins are available for lodging on select weekends

over the winter. (888) 896-3818; www.olympicnationalparks.com/accommodations/
lake-crescent-resort.aspx. GPS: N48 03.438'/W123 48.002'

Sol Duc Hot Springs Resort, Olympic National Park, WA: With three soaking pools fed by natural hot springs with water ranging in temperature from 99 to
104 degrees Fahrenheit, the Sol Duc Hot Springs Resort is a great place to soak
your weary bones after the loop hike to Sol Duc Falls and Lover's Lane Falls. You
can stay overnight in one of the resort's thirty-three cabins ($116–$321) or just use
the soaking pools (and adjacent locker room and showers) for $11.50. The attached
restaurant serves up hearty fare at reasonable prices. Open March through October
only. 12076 Sol Duc Hot Springs Rd., Port Angeles, WA 98363; (888) 896-3818; www
.olympicnationalparks.com/accommodations/sol-duc-hot-springs-resort.aspx. GPS:
N47 58.176'/W123 51.812'

Sol Duc Campground, Olympic National Park, WA: Eighty-one tent/RV sites
($14/night). Car campers at this bare-bones national park campground can hike right
to Sol Duc Falls and Lover's Lane Falls from their campsite. Open year-round (flush
toilets and potable water only May-September). From Port Angeles, WA, take US
101 west for 27.5 miles and turn left (south) onto Sol Duc Hot Springs Road and
follow it for 12.5 miles to the campground entrance on the right (west) side of the
road just beyond Sol Duc Hot Springs Resort. (360) 565-3130; www.nps.gov/olym/
planyourvisit/campgrounds.htm. GPS: N47 58.007'/W123 51.480'

1 Beaver Falls

Anyone traveling to the northwest section of the Olympic Peninsula should be sure to check out Beaver Falls, where Beaver Creek crashes over a 70-foot-wide rock wall and lands 25 feet below in a cozy little woodland pool.

Start: Dirt parking pull-out along east side of WA 113 (Burnt Mountain Road), 1.9 miles north of the junction with US 101. GPS: N48 05.651'/W124 16.017'
Height: 25 feet
Difficulty: Moderate
Approximate hiking time: 10 minutes
Distance: 0.1 mile out and back

Trail surface: Wet trail through brush
County: Clallam
Land status: National forest
Trail contact: Olympic National Forest, Pacific Ranger District, Forks, WA; www.fs.usda.gov/olympic; (360) 374-6522
Maps: DeLorme *Washington Atlas & Gazetteer*. Page 28 E3

Finding the trailhead: Take US 101 to the town of Sappho and then head north on WA 113 (Burnt Mountain Road). Follow WA 113 north for 1.9 miles and as it starts to curve to the right, look for a large dirt pull-out parking area along the right (east) side of the road where the guardrail gives way.

The Hike

Getting down to the base of Beaver Falls from the unmarked parking area up above takes less than 5 minutes, but it involves picking your way down a steep, rocky, slick bank trail—there will be slipping involved and use caution not to fall or sprain an

Just a hop, skip, and a jump from WA 113, Beaver Falls provides a serene setting in the heart of the Olympic Peninsula.

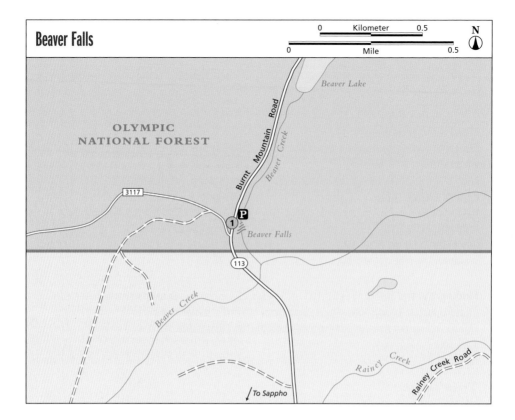

Beaver Falls

OLYMPIC NATIONAL FOREST

Beaver Lake

Burnt Mountain Road

Beaver Creek

3117

P

1

Beaver Falls

113

Beaver Creek

Rainey Creek

Rainey Creek Road

To Sappho

ankle. The trail bottoms out at a small pool at the base of Beaver Falls, where Beaver Creek free falls for 25 feet over a sheer rock ledge. In winter and spring, the entire 70-foot-wide expanse of Beaver Falls spills water, but in summer and fall less flow means the falls split up into three braids. While the pool below the falls looks like a nice place to take a dip, would-be swimmers should think twice about jumping in given contaminants in the water from upstream mining and logging operations. Return the way you came to get back up to the parking area, then wander 70 feet to the north to check out the top of the falls.

Miles and Directions

0.0 From the unmarked trailhead (GPS: N48 05.651'/W124 16.017') behind the guardrail, pick your way down through what looks like a game trail through thick brush.

300' Arrive at the pool at the base of Beaver Falls. Enjoy the serenity and then turn around and head back up the way you came.

0.1 Return to the trailhead.

2 Sol Duc Falls/Lover's Lane Falls

Sol Duc Falls may be one of the most famous waterfalls in the state of Washington, and for good reason. The Sol Duc River puts on quite a show when it braids into four channels that then plunge side-by-side over a sharp ledge and fall 37 feet straight down into a deep, dark chasm below. Then the accumulated river falls another 11 feet into another larger gorge before shuttling on downstream. Hikers willing to make the 0.8-mile trek through otherworldly old-growth forest can view the spectacle from a high wooden footbridge, under which the freshly fallen river quickly passes. Turning around and heading back to the parking lot is one option, but even better is turning the excursion into a 5.5-mile loop hike past some of the largest Sitka spruce and western red cedar trees on the planet on the way past lovely Lover's Lane Falls upriver from Sol Duc Falls.

Start: Trailhead kiosk at dead end of Sol Duc Hot Springs Road. GPS: N47 57.296' / W123 50.084'

Height: Sol Duc Falls: 48 feet over two sections; Lover's Lane Falls: 53 feet

Difficulty: Easy/Moderate

Approximate hiking time: 1–3 hours

Distance: 1.6 miles out and back; or 5.5 miles via the loop on the Lover's Lane Trail

Trail surface: Well-maintained dirt hiking trail with occasional rocks and roots

County: Clallam

Land status: National park

Trail contact: Olympic National Park, Port Angeles, WA; www.nps.gov/olym; (360) 565-3130

Maps: DeLorme *Washington Atlas & Gazetteer*: Page 43 A6

Finding the trailhead: Follow Sol Duc Hot Springs Road 13.5 miles from its junction with US 101 to its terminus at the Sol Duc Falls trailhead. (In winter, the road is closed at the Sol Doc Hot Springs Resort, adding 1.5 miles to the hike.)

The Hike

Drive to the end of Sol Duc Hot Springs Road and park. The trailhead is well marked with kiosks bearing information on backcountry travel in general and maps outlining the trails fanning out from the Sol Duc drainage. Within 150 feet of the trailhead, a series of twenty-eight stair steps heading downhill makes things easy. The surrounding landscape is a classic example of a temperate old-growth forest: Age-old nurse logs give birth to lines of smaller trees; fungus, moss, and lichens inhabit every possible niche; epiphytes (hanging "air" plants that get their nutrients from the sun and wind) hang off the boughs of small Sitka spruce trees and larger big-leaf maples; bunchberry, sword fern, salmonberry, and devil's club crowd the edges of the trail.

At about a half mile into the hike, after crossing over the third of many small wooden footbridges, you can start to hear the sounds of the rushing river—the

Sol Duc Falls, accessible via a short hike through quintessential old-growth temperate rain forest, is one of the most scenic cascades in the Pacific Northwest.

waterfall isn't in sight yet but can't be far off. Cross another wooden footbridge and go right at the trail sign toward Sol Duc Falls and Lover's Lane. The Sol Duc River finally comes into view downhill and to the right, with a rough-hewn timber fence protecting hikers from falling into the river gorge.

Making your way downhill, stop to marvel at the Canyon Creek Shelter, a 25-by-12-foot log cabin with a dirt floor and an open front wall with a covered firepit. The shelter was built by FDR's Civilian Conservation Corps in 1939 to "enhance the safety of visitors" to the newly created national park. An information sheet posted inside sheds light on the building's original purpose: "As an early Olympic National Park hiker, imagine how happy you would have been to find this shelter after walking in the heavy rain wearing heavy cotton and wool clothing and perhaps carrying a cumbersome wood, leather, and canvas backpack!"

Past the shelter, the trail winds down some more wooden stair steps and eventually bottoms out at a magnificent 25-foot-long wooden footbridge high over the gorge at the bottom of Sol Duc Falls. Walk halfway across the bridge and look left to see Sol Duc Falls in all of its four-tailed glory. To the right look down and see the river rushing downstream through a tight canyon. Cross over the bridge and take in Sol Duc Falls from some additional vantage points. After exploring the vicinity of Sol Duc Falls some more, it's decision time: go back the way you came (making for a 1.6-mile out and back hike), or see some new terrain and another jaw-dropper of a waterfall by looping around on the Lover's Lane Trail (for a 5.5-mile hike).

To get to the Lover's Lane Trail, hikers crossing over the bridge at Sol Duc Falls should turn right (west) and look for the trail sign marking the way to Lover's Lane/Sol Duc Hot Springs Resort. The narrow and gnarled Lover's Lane Trail makes the Sol Duc Falls Trail look downright civilized as hikers must watch their steps carefully. Massive uplifted root structures of fallen old-growth trees stand as testament to the power of nature—and a reminder to stay away from the forest during stormy weather.

After another 0.2 mile of slogging through the rough trail and drinking in the splendor of forest primeval, the sound of rushing water fills the ears and soon enough the trail funnels itself onto another large, rough-hewn wooden footbridge that utilizes one big log with its top shaved flat to facilitate walking to cover the 50-foot span across Canyon Creek. To the left slightly upstream is a smaller waterfall and to the right downstream is Lover's Lane Falls.

What makes Lover's Lane Falls unique is the fact that two huge boulders, each the size of a small cabin, at the top of a cliff break the path of the Sol Duc River into two rushing braids. A huge fallen old-growth tree is broken in two like a matchstick and stuck against one of the boulders thanks to years of water pressure bearing down on it. One braid of the river goes off to the right and falls into a relatively calm swirling pool about 20 feet below on top of a smaller cliff before dropping off again into oblivion below. The other braid shifts off to the left and takes a 53-foot plunge into the unseen gorge below. After exploring Lover's Lane Falls fully, hikers should cross

Looking upstream at Sol Duc Falls from an outcropping off the trail

the footbridge and take the side trail to the left to check out the Upper Falls, which veil out across a wide rock wall and fall 13 feet.

Hikers looking to save energy can turn around and return the way they came for a 2.2-mile out and back hike or continue on the Lover's Lane Trail and loop back around on another section of the Sol Duc Falls trail, making for a 5.5-mile hike all told. Either way, abundant groves of iconic Pacific Northwest old-growth trees throughout the area make traveling through on foot a feast for the eyes.

Miles and Directions

0.0 Trailhead kiosk (GPS: N47 57.296' / W123 50.084') at dead end of Sol Duc Hot Springs Road.

0.1 Cross a small stream on a rough-hewn wooden footbridge, one of many along the trail.

0.5 After crossing the third wooden footbridge of the hike, the sound of rushing water comes into the soundscape; the waterfall can't be far!

0.7 After crossing a fourth wooden footbridge, look for the Canyon Creek Shelter straight ahead and then go right at the trail junction toward Sol Duc Falls (trail sign marks the way).

0.8 Arrive at Sol Duc Falls (GPS: N47 57.113' / W123 49.184'), viewable from large wooden footbridge over gorge and viewing areas on other side of the bridge. (If you're not continuing on to make a 5.5-mile loop via the Lover's Lane Trail, return the way you came for a 1.6-mile hike.)

Sol Duc Falls/Lover's Lane Falls

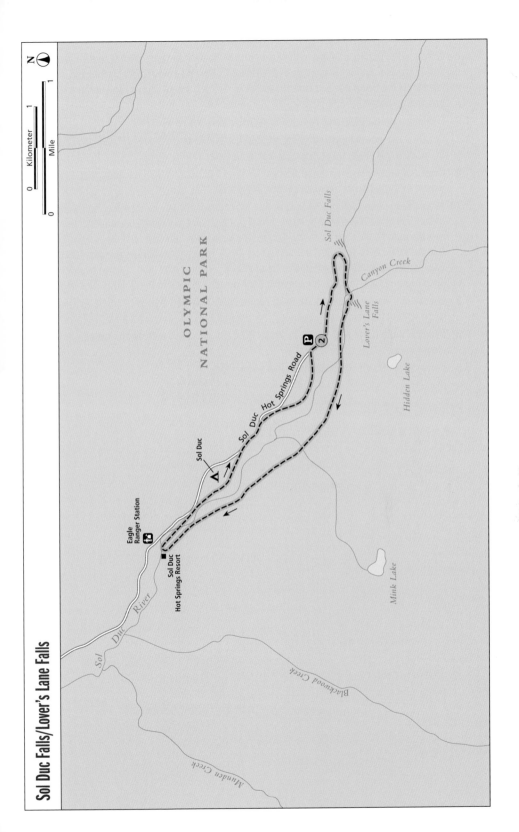

0.9 Cross the Sol Duc Falls Bridge to the south side of the river and take the trail to the right, keeping an eye out for the trail sign (GPS: N47 57.068'/W123 49.258') marking the junction of the Deer Lake and Lover's Lane trails. Go right toward Lover's Lane and Sol Duc Hot Springs Resort.

1.1 Footbridge over Lover's Lane Falls (GPS: N47 57.054'/W123 49.596').

2.1 Groves of old-growth forest, including huge spruce burl trees (GPS: N47 57.198'/W123 50.582') with a single burl around 20 feet in diameter.

2.9 Cross ~300-foot-long wooden footbridge (GPS: N47 57.622'/W123 51.284') that curves around to the right over a marshy section of the trail.

3.75 At a signed junction with the Mink Lake Trail, stay right on the Lover's Lane Trail, and follow down for another 200 feet to the back of Sol Duc Hot Springs Resort. Locate and cross over the automobile bridge over the Sol Duc River and then turn right onto the marked Sol Duc Falls trail (GPS: N47 58.196'/W123 51.765'), keeping the river to your right. The trail then winds in and out of Sol Duc Campground for a half mile (and is partially paved). Keep heading east and look for sporadic signs pointing the way to the Sol Duc Falls Trail.

4.2 Check out the massive old-growth Sitka spruce (GPS: N47 58.035'/W123 51.553') just to the right of the trail.

5.0 Beautiful grove (GPS: N47 57.327'/W123 50.476') of iconic Pacific Northwest old-growth trees.

5.5 Return to the Sol Duc Falls trailhead and parking area.

3 Marymere Falls

A short hike through majestic temperate rain forest leads to sublime views of 119-foot Marymere Falls, where Falls Creek cuts through a high cliff notch and horsetails down for the upper half of its drop before fanning out into a mossy green amphitheater below. While you won't likely be alone—Marymere Falls is one of the top attractions within Olympic National Park—it's well worth a stop and the short hike to get there.

Start: Storm King Ranger Station on Barnes Point, Olympic National Park. GPS: N48 03.474'/W123 47.305'
Height: 119 feet
Difficulty: Easy/Moderate
Approximate hiking time: 1-2 hours
Distance: 1.6 miles round-trip, lollipop route (out and back with a loop at the terminus)

Trail surface: Well-maintained dirt hiking trail with occasional rocks and roots, and timber stair steps on some steep sections
County: Clallam
Land status: National park
Trail contact: Olympic National Park, Port Angeles, WA; www.nps.gov/olym; (360) 565-3130
Maps: DeLorme *Washington Atlas & Gazetteer:* Page 29 E7

Finding the trailhead: From US 101 about 20 miles west of Port Angeles, turn north onto Lake Crescent Road, and take the first right (east), following signs to the parking area at the Storm King Ranger Station. Park and walk toward the quaint old ranger station building's front porch to access the marked trailhead.

The Hike

Starting out from the trailhead at Storm King Ranger Station (GPS: N48 03.474'/W123 47.305'), the trail meanders down to the shoreline of Crescent Lake—a nice place to indulge in a cool dip on a hot day—before crossing through a round metal culvert foot tunnel under US 101. After walking through the tunnel, stay right toward Marymere Falls at a signed junction (GPS: N48 03.144'/W123 47.322') with the Barnes Creek Trail. Cross one then another footbridge over Barnes Creek, keeping an eye out for some of grandest old-growth western red cedar trees on the planet. Then start ascending on well-maintained rough-hewn stair steps up to a ridge. Look for views (and listen for the sounds of rushing water) off to the left of the lower and section of Marymere Falls. Keep zig-zagging up via a series of three switchbacks. Then head left at the signed "Falls Loop" junction.

Within 100 feet, check out the lower viewpoint of the Marymere Falls, then continue up another series of stair steps that dead-ends at a fenced overlook that yields views of the middle and upper sections of Marymere Falls. After snapping a few pics,

Views of Marymere Falls are quite the reward after the short but heart-pounding hike up from the shores of Olympic National Park's Lake Crescent.

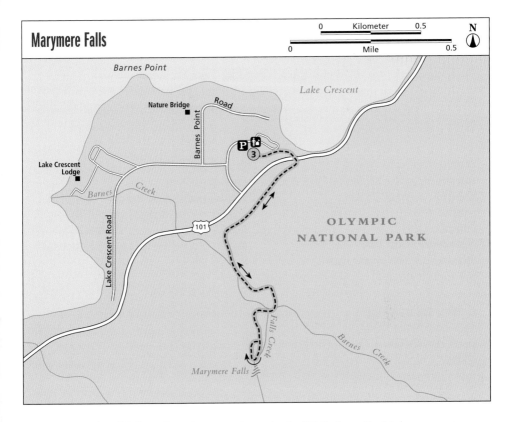

Marymere Falls

turn around and follow the other way down in the "Falls Loop," which starts out as a steep trail and eventually turns into more stair steps before rejoining the main lower section of the trail that leads back to the trailhead and parking lot.

Miles and Directions

0.0 Trailhead (GPS: N48 03.474'/W123 47.305') at Storm King Ranger Station.

0.1 Pass by shore of Lake Crescent and head through foot tunnel under US 101.

0.4 At junction with Lake Crescent Lodge Trail, stay straight (south) toward Marymere Falls.

0.5 At junction with Mt. Storm King Trail, stay straight (south) toward Marymere Falls.

0.6 At junction with Barnes Creek Trail, stay straight (south) toward Marymere Falls Trail, then cross over Barnes Creek on one footbridge and then Falls Creek on another footbridge.

0.7 At marked junction of Falls Loop, go left and uphill to the first overlook of Marymere Falls.

0.8 Continue on to the upper overlook of Marymere Falls. Take in the view of the upper section of the falls and then continue down steeply to the Falls Loop junction and then retrace your steps back to the trailhead.

1.6 Arrive back at the trailhead.

4 Madison Creek Falls

Madison Creek Falls' 76-foot horsetail drop into a perfect woodland pool is an awe-inspiring scene; all the better that it is easily accessible via a relatively flat, paved, 250-foot trail through the forest at the base of Olympic National Park's wild and woolly Elwha River drainage.

Start: Madison Creek Falls parking area off east side of Olympic Hot Springs Road. GPS: N48 02.467'/W123 35.394'
Height: 76 feet
Difficulty: Easy
Approximate hiking time: 10 minutes
Distance: 500 feet out and back
Trail surface: Paved

County: Clallam
Land status: National park
Trail contact: Olympic National Park, Port Angeles, WA; www.nps.gov/olym; (360) 565-3130
Maps: DeLorme *Washington Atlas & Gazetteer*: Page 29 E9

Finding the trailhead: From its junction with US 101 some 8.5 miles west of Port Angeles, follow Olympic Hot Springs Road south for 2 miles to the Madison Falls parking area on the left (east). Entrance may require Olympic National Park admission fee ($15/week or $30/year per vehicle).

The Hike

Pick up the marked, paved trail by the small parking area and follow it as it winds into the side of the gorge and terminates at an overlook right below Madison Falls. Those

A close-up view of Madison Falls' initial drop

One of the most accessible of the Olympic Peninsula's cascades, Madison Falls tumbles 76 feet into a verdant gorge.

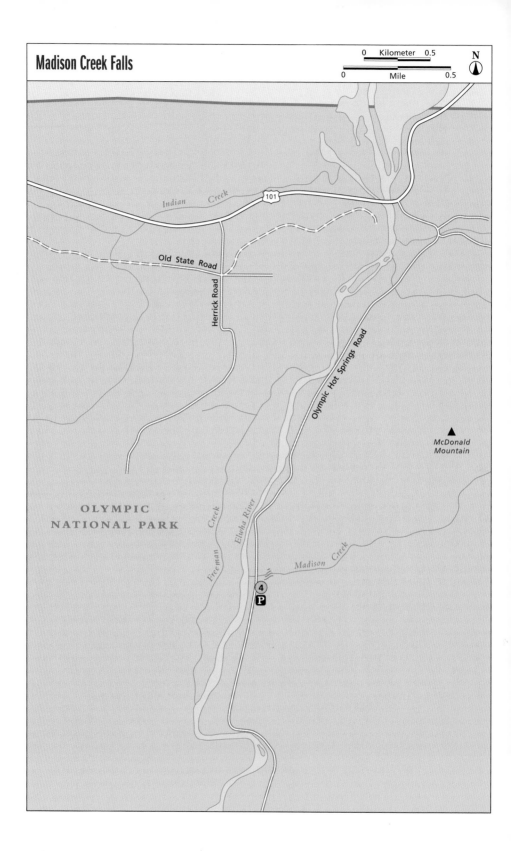

Madison Creek Falls

A RIVER REBORN: RESTORING THE ELWHA

Olympic National Park has been in the news a lot lately thanks to the largest dam removal project in the history of the world along the Elwha River there, not far from Madison Falls. The massive undertaking to remove the two antiquated hydroelectric dams and restore a once-upon-a-time thriving wild riparian ecosystem along the Elwha started in 2011 and took 3 years to complete. According to members of the Lower Elwha Klallam Tribe, whose ancestors lived by the river for thousands of years, the Elwha was home to some of the healthiest salmon runs on the West Coast before the dams went in starting in 1910. Nowadays, scientists are amazed at how quickly the riparian environment is reverting to its former glory, even though the dams had been in place for more than a century: Salmon are migrating past the former dam sites while trees and shrubs are putting down roots in the drained reservoir beds. It's an exciting time to visit the Elwha drainage if you are in the area anyway, so make sure to save some time to check out the former Elwha Dam view and access (GPS: N48 05.883' / W123 32.756') and former Lake Mills access (GPS: N47 58.447' / W123 35.511') sites.

interested in a closer look, or wanting to splash around in the spray, can venture into the pool at the bottom of the falls—but beware, glacial-fed Madison Creek is cold!

Miles and Directions

0.0 Start at the marked trailhead (GPS: N48 02.467' / W123 35.394') by the Madison Creek Falls parking lot off Olympic Hot Springs Road.

250' Arrive at Madison Creek Falls overlook. Return the way you came.

500' Arrive back at the trailhead.

5 Murhut Falls

Murhut Falls, long a secret only known to locals along the east side of the Olympic Peninsula, cascades 153 feet in two sections down into a verdant gorge along the Duckabush River, culminating in a small pool festooned with fallen old-growth logs. Adventurers can wander into the pool at the base of the lower falls and cool off in the glacier-fed spray. This classic Northwest waterfall is accessible via a short hike and is well worth a visit for anyone traveling on the east side of the Olympic Peninsula.

Start: "Murhut Falls Trail" sign at trailhead off FR 2510. GPS: N47 40.592' / W123 02.319'
Height: 153 feet over two sections
Difficulty: Easy/Moderate
Approximate hiking time: 30 minutes
Distance: 1.6 miles out and back
Trail surface: Well-maintained dirt hiking trail free of roots and rocks

County: Jefferson
Land status: National forest
Trail contact: Olympic National Forest, Hood Canal Ranger District, Quilcene, WA; www .fs.usda.gov/recarea/olympic/recreation/ recarea/?recid=47691; (360) 765-2200
Maps: DeLorme *Washington Atlas & Gazetteer.* Page 44 4D

Finding the trailhead: From US 101 Brinnon, WA, drive northwest on Duckabush Road for 3.5 miles where it turns into FR 2510 (and becomes dirt in the process). Continue on for another 2.5 miles to a fork; head right (north), following signs for Murhut Falls. Drive another 1.5 miles and park in the pull-out to the left (south); the well-marked trailhead is on the right (north) side of the road.

The Hike

Hiking to Murhut Falls takes 15 to 20 minutes and is well worth the slight amount of elevation gain (175 feet) encountered. The trail, which is wide, even, and well-graded, was refurbished in recent years by the Forest Service, making access to this gem of a woodland waterfall that much easier. Right from the trailhead, which is marked with a "Murhut Falls Trail" sign, hikers enter into another world dominated by big trees. A hundred feet in, a trail register kiosk beckons hikers to sign in and out of the hike. Then for a third of a mile the trail climbs, with classic second-growth forest views punctuated by winding mossy big-leaf maple boughs, pink rhododendron blossoms, yellow-orange salmonberries, and crumbling old-growth nurse log. The trail then flattens out and rounds a curve to the left, at which point the sound of rushing water starts to dominate the soundscape. In another hundred feet, the Duckabush River comes into view for the first time, and soon thereafter hikers are treated to peekaboo views of Murhut Falls.

While Rocky Brook Falls is accessible year-round, locals flock there on hot summer days to cool off in its refreshing mists.

CAN WATERFALLS REALLY MAKE YOU HAPPY?

There just may be some truth to the rumor that being around waterfalls can uplift your mood, thanks to the so-called "negative ions" pervasive in such environments. The collision of water molecules with each other, such as at a waterfall or an ocean beach, causes the water to become positively charged, and the surrounding air to be negatively charged.

According to Pierce J. Howard, PhD, author of *The Owner's Manual for the Brain: Everyday Applications from Mind-Brain Research*, it makes sense that waterfalls can make you feel good, given that negative ions hitting our bloodstream can produce biochemical reactions linked to alleviating depression, relieving stress, and boosting energy.

"High concentrations of negative ions are essential for high energy and positive mood," he reports. "Negative ions suppress serotonin levels in much the same way that natural sunlight suppresses melatonin. Hence the invigorating effect of fresh air and sunshine and the correspondingly depressed feelings associated with being closed in and dark.

"The atmosphere we breathe normally is full of positive and negative ions," he adds. "Air-conditioning, lack of ventilation, and long dry spells remove negative ions.

"The best ratios of negative to positive ions are associated with waterfalls and the time before, during, and after storms," says Howard. "The worst are found in windowless rooms and closed, moving vehicles."

In case you needed another reason to get up off the couch or office chair and out into the woods on a waterfall hike, now you have it. You'll be sharper. You'll be more productive. You'll be invigorated. You'll be happier. It's all about the negative ions. Now go, off to the trailhead . . .

Miles and Directions

0.0 Trailhead (GPS: N47 43.137' / W122 56.609') is around a road gate that allows maintenance vehicles access to the hydroelectric facility on Rocky Brook.

0.1 A chain-link fence over the hydroelectric outlet protects hikers from falling into river (a sign there reads: "Danger Keep Off: This Area Subject to Sudden Stream Flow Changes"), and offers a first glimpse of the waterfall up ahead. The road turns into a rocky trail and approaches the base of the falls.

0.2 Huge boulders and fallen logs dominate the scene at the base of Rocky Brook Falls. Poking around this otherworldly landscape is mandatory, but watch out as all surfaces are slippery due to the constant spray coming off the falls. After relishing in the wet and wild environment around the base of the falls, return to the car via the same path.

0.4 Arrive back at the trailhead.

7 Falls View Falls

Falls View Falls is a narrow ribbon of water (averaging just 5 feet wide) dropping down a verdant, nearly vertical cliff into Quilcene Canyon some 200 feet below. While it's hard to get up close, the view from the Falls View Loop Trail across Quilcene Canyon gives an almost aerial perspective. The fall emerges from a clifftop and then bisects a sea of green on its straight and narrow course to the canyon floor below. While the loop trail isn't much of a hike, easy access from US 101 makes it well worth a quick stop.

See map on p. 28.
Start: "Falls View Loop" trail sign at far end of west campground loop. GPS: N47 47.373' / W122 55.712'
Height: 200 feet
Difficulty: Easy
Approximate hiking time: 10 minutes
Distance: 0.1 mile, loop
Trail surface: Well-maintained dirt trail

County: Jefferson
Land status: National forest
Trail contact: Olympic National Forest, Hood Canal Ranger District, Quilcene, WA; www.fs.usda.gov/recarea/olympic/recreation/recarea/?recid=47691; (360) 765-2200
Maps: DeLorme *Washington Atlas & Gazetteer*. Page 44 5C

Finding the trailhead: Take US 101 to Falls View Campground (south of Quilcene, WA). If campground (and road gate) is open, drive the loop to the left and park at the day-use area at the far end. If the gate is locked, park outside it and walk the quarter mile to the trailhead, where a sign indicates the Falls View Loop Trail #848 starts off to the right.

The Hike

Even though it may be short as far as hikes go, the walk to check out Falls View Falls packs a punch. The single-track trail ducks into heavy second-growth forest at its start and then soon takes hikers to the rim of Quilcene Canyon. A tall chain-link fence protects people (and pets) from falling hundreds of feet into the canyon below. After 100 feet of flat hiking, the views open up across Quilcene Canyon to Falls View Falls, a ribbon of milky white bisecting an otherwise green canopy–encrusted canyon wall. A small viewing spot juts out from the main trail, offering up a panorama sure to make anyone feel small. After taking it all in, hikers can duck back into the forest to return to the trailhead and parking area. Those looking for more exercise can go down the Falls View Canyon Trail #868, a 1.3-mile loop down into the canyon.

Getting up close involves a rigorous hike and some bushwhacking, so most people check out Falls View Falls from across the canyon.

Miles and Directions

0.0 Trailhead (GPS: N47 47.373'/W122 55.712') is at the day-use parking area on left loop of Falls View Campground. Trail dips into second-growth forest.

150' As trees give way to the cliff-side and a chain-link fence, Falls View Falls comes into view.

250' Trail juts out from edge to offer panoramic views of Quilcene Canyon punctuated by Falls View Falls in the middle.

400' Trail leaves edge of canyon and loops back into forest.

0.1 Arrive back at the trailhead.

Honorable Mentions

A. Spoon Creek Falls, Olympic National Forest, WA

This gem of a waterfall may be a little off the beaten path—some 37 miles off US 101 on a part-gravel road up the wild Wynoochee Valley—but is well worth a visit for those on the south side of the Olympic Peninsula. Hike the marked Spoon Creek Falls trail down 0.2 miles to its terminus in a forest dale dominated by Douglas fir and vine maple trees, then walk upstream and around the turn in the river to see the falls from its base. Watch your step on wet, slippery rocks and bring a walking stick if you need one. To get to Spoon Creek Falls from WA 12 near the town of Montesano, drive north on the Wynoochee Valley Road (which eventually turns into FR 22) and follow it for 34 miles. Then turn right on FR 23 and go another 2.6 miles to the trailhead just past a small bridge over the West Fork Satsop River. Waterfall lovers can make a day of it by driving around the maze of forest roads south of Wynoochee Lake to check out nearby Wynoochee Falls and Perfection Falls. GPS: N47 21.220'/W123 33.888'

B. Hamma Hamma Falls, Olympic National Forest, WA

Falling 25 feet into an upper punchbowl and then plunging another 50 feet into a deep, ferny gorge, Hamma Hamma Falls is a welcome sight after driving more than 13 miles on the wild and woolly Hamma Hamma Road into the heart of the Olympic National Forest. Fishermen should consider hiking into the Mildred Lakes from the waterfall for some of the best freshwater fishing in the state. From US 101 south of Brinnon, WA, drive west on Hamma Hamma Road (FR 25) for 6.4 miles and follow it right at a T-junction (toward Lena Creek) just past Hamma Hamma Campground and Cabin Creek Road. Continue for about 7 more miles to the bridge over the Hamma Hamma River and park at the road's terminus. Listen and look for Hamma Hamma Falls—it's hard to miss—right before the Mildred Lakes trailhead. GPS: N47 34.542'/W123 15.570'

C. Merriman Falls, Olympic National Park, WA

Shooting off a rocky cliff and then veiling out over a 40-foot falls before S-curving through a mossy green tangle of rocks and fallen logs before crossing under the road on its way to its confluence with the mighty Quinault River, Merriman Falls is a must-see for nature lovers traversing the Quinault region of the Olympic Peninsula. From US 101 south of Lake Quinault, drive 6 miles northwest on Quinault Lake

South Shore Road and look for the waterfall to the south from the bridge over Merriman Creek. Park along the side of the road and walk down to check out the grotto-like atmosphere at the base of the pretty falls. GPS: N47 30.016'/W123 47.054'

D. Enchanted Valley, Olympic National Park, WA

Also known as the Valley of 10,000 Waterfalls, this remote section of the Olympic Peninsula's wild interior features thousands of seasonal waterfalls fed by spring snow-melt from the high peaks all around it, and as such is one of the premier backpacking destinations in the Pacific Northwest. From US 101 south of Lake Quinault, drive 17 miles northwest on Quinault Lake South Shore Road and then follow signs for Graves Creek Campground. Park there and don your backpack and hiking boots to embark on the 13-mile hike into the Enchanted Valley. (Free backcountry camping permits are required for overnight stays in the park's wilderness areas and can be obtained on the way in from the Quinault Wilderness Information Office on Quinault Lake South Shore Road, next to Lake Quinault Lodge 2 miles north of US 101.) GPS: N47 40.308'/W123 23.277'

E. Strawberry Bay Falls, Olympic National Park, WA

The most prominent waterfall in the state that plunges off a cliff directly into the ocean, Strawberry Bay Falls (also known as Third Beach Falls) tumbles 119 feet over two horsetail tiers into the surf of Olympic National Park's wild and woolly Pacific coastline. While driftwood- and seastack-festooned Third Beach is scenic any time of year, waterfall lovers will want to make the pilgrimage in late winter or early spring, as the Strawberry Bay Falls usually dries up by May or June. From Forks, drive about 12 miles west on WA 110 (La Push Road), staying left at the major forks in the road toward La Push (not Mora), and look for the Third Beach trailhead and a few parking spaces on the left (south); then hike the easy 1.3-mile trail through otherworldly coastal temperate rain forest down to Third Beach and look for Strawberry Bay Falls about a half mile to the south. GPS: N47 52.378'/W124 34.628'

Northwest Washington

Northwest Washington is a land of extremes. Down at sea level, the San Juan Islands offer direct access to the chilly, teeming waters of the Pacific—much to the delight of beachgoers, kayakers, fishermen, and whale watchers—along with a good measure of quaint island culture (think B&Bs with homespun quilts and restaurants specializing in slow food). Meanwhile, thousands of feet higher in elevation but only 50 miles east as the crow flies, the

The glaciated peaks of the North Cascades are known as America's Alps.

classic glaciated peaks and valleys of Mt. Baker and the North Cascades (nicknamed America's Alps for their likeness to Western Europe's iconic mountain range) challenge hikers, paddlers, backpackers, and campers to get vertiginous, exploring over hill and dale.

While the San Juans and North Cascades may seem worlds apart topographically (let alone culturally), they are more similar than you would expect geologically, with the same bedrock underpinnings throughout. Tectonic forces account for the elevation differences between the two regions, but similar patterns of volcanic flows and ice-age glaciation underscore that Northwest Washington is really just one big geological neighborhood.

Waterfall lovers will particularly appreciate getting to know this neighborhood, given that it's home to thousands of cascades across millions of acres of untrammeled forest. Whether you're deep in a forest grotto in the San Juan Islands staring down at pretty little Cascade Falls or gazing up between monolithic cliff walls in North Cascades National Park at 2,568-foot Colonial Creek Falls, you'll be glad you made the trip.

Camping and Accommodations

Moran State Park, Orcas Island, WA: 151 tent sites ($20–$31) across five different camping areas within this 5,500-acre park. You can hike within the park to Cascade Falls as well as other nearby points of interest (like Mountain Lake and the summit of Mt. Constitution). From the East Sound ferry terminal on Orcas Island, drive around the island for 14 miles on the main island road and then turn left (east) onto Mt. Constitution Road to enter the state park. (360) 376-2326; www.parks.wa.gov/547/Moran. GPS: N48 38.963'/W122 50.791'

Rosario Resort, Orcas Island, WA: Offers a wide range of accommodation options ranging from hotel-style rooms to condos with kitchens to guestrooms overlooking the marina ($189–$499). The central location allows for easy access to all the charms of Orcas Island including nearby Moran State Park with the lookout from Mt. Constitution and the hike down to Cascade Falls. (360) 376-2222, www.rosarioresort.com. GPS: N48 38.676'/W122 52.395'

Douglas Fir Campground, Mt. Baker-Snoqualmie National Forest, WA: This car campground off WA 542 has thirty sites for tents or RVs along with vault toilets and hand-pump wells. Makes for a good base camp for waterfall hunters interested in checking out Nooksack Falls, Heliotrope Falls, Racehorse Falls, and others in the Mt. Baker watershed. Open May through September. Some sites can be reserved in advance through recreation.gov. (877) 444-6777, www.fs.usda.gov/recarea/mbs/recreation/camping-cabins/recarea/?recid=17580&actid=29. GPS: N48 54.157'/W121 54.942'

Colonial Creek Campground, North Cascades National Park, WA: This National Park Service car campground with 142 tent/RV sites ($12/night) is centrally located right off WA 20 in the heart of the North Cascades where Colonial

Creek meets Diablo Lake. Easy access to Colonial Creek Falls, with Rainy Lake Falls, Gorge Creek Falls, Ladder Creek Falls, and Cedar Hollow Falls not too far off. Flush toilets; garbage and recycling; potable water; first-come, first-served (no reservations). Open May through September www.nps.gov/noca/planyourvisit/camping .htm. GPS: N48 41.345'/W121 05.731'

Gorge Lake Campground, Diablo, WA: This free campground on the shores of Gorge Lake below one of Seattle City Light's three dams on the Skagit River only has six sites available on a first-come, first-served basis. Vault toilets; no water or garbage services. Easy access to North Cascades National Park including Gorge Creek Falls, Ladder Creek Falls, and Rainy Lake Falls, not to mention Ross Lake and Diablo Lake. GPS: N48 42.947'/W121 09.096'

Buffalo Run Inn, Marblemount, WA: This comfy bed-and-breakfast–style inn off WA 20—formerly a roadhouse catering to the thirsts of gold miners, mountain men, and lumberjacks—now has fifteen guestrooms ($59–$85/night) and a hearty restaurant across the street. It's a great place to enjoy the comforts of civilization after a few days of roughing it in and around North Cascades National Park. (360) 873-2103, www.buffaloruninn.com. GPS: N48 31.623'/W121 25.882'

The Freestone Inn, Mazama, WA: The most luxurious digs around the Methow Valley, this historic inn has thirty-six deluxe rooms/cabins ($165–$225/night), each with its own private veranda/deck, fireplace, and forest view. Easy access to the Methow Valley trail system—if you didn't bring your own mountain bike or cross-country ski gear, you can rent it on site. Cedar Falls hike nearby. (509) 996-3906, www.freestoneinn.com. GPS: N48 35.751'/W120 26.348'

The Rolling Huts, Mazama, WA: This "herd" of six small cabins ($135/night) in a valley near the Methow River—designed by Thomas Kundig, one of the leading lights of Seattle's modern architecture scene—may be the most stylish place to overnight in the Methow Valley. Each "rolling hut" sleeps three to four comfortably but couples will appreciate it most. Open year-round. If you can't get a "hut," try one of the summer-only platform tents 500 feet away. (509) 996-4442, www.rollinghuts .com. GPS: N48 32.961'/W120 20.299'

Early Winters Campground, Mazama, WA: This bare-bones Forest Service campground offers up twelve sites ($8/night) at the confluence of Early Winters Creek and the Methow River. Close to Goat Wall (rock climbers rejoice), the "town" of Mazama, and the Cedar Falls hike. Vault toilet; potable water; garbage services; first-come, first-served (no reservations). Open April through November. www.fs.usda .gov/recarea/okawen/recreation/camping-cabins/recarea/?recid=59203&actid=31. GPS: N48 41.345'/W121 05.731'

8 Cascade Falls

As if homespun island culture, breaching orca whales, driftwood-studded beaches, and the view from towering Mt. Constitution aren't enough to occupy your time when visiting Orcas Island in Northwest Washington's San Juan archipelago, there is always the short hike through forest primeval to Cascade Falls. The 41-foot cataract in Moran State Park drops from a chasm in Cascade Creek and then fans out before finishing in a small gorge criss-crossed by huge fallen big-leaf maple and western red cedar trees. This misty, mossy fairy domain is a great place to visit with kids, who will love climbing around on fallen logs and playing in the spray of the falls.

Start: Marked trailhead on the south side of Cascade Falls parking lot off Mt. Constitution Road in Moran State Park. GPS: N48 38.905'/W122 49.961'
Height: 41 feet
Difficulty: Easy but some sloping trail and stair steps
Approximate hiking time: 30 minutes
Distance: 0.6 mile out and back (or loop option with same distance)

Trail surface: Dirt trail with lots of roots, some rough-hewn stair steps
County: San Juan
Land status: State park
Trail contact: Washington State Parks, Moran State Park, Orcas Island, WA; www.parks.wa .gov/547/Moran; (360) 376-2326
Maps: DeLorme *Washington Atlas & Gazetteer.* Page 15 6D

Finding the trailhead: From the ferry dock in East Sound on Orcas Island, follow the main road around the island for 14 miles (it becomes Main Street then Crescent Beach Drive then Olga Road along the way) and turn left (east) onto Mt. Constitution Road, which heads uphill into Moran State Park for a quarter mile to the marked Cascade Falls parking lot and trailhead (GPS: N48 38.905'/W122 49.961') on the right (south). (See www.wsdot.wa.gov/ferries for information on ferry service between Orcas and Anacortes on the mainland.)

The Hike

From the signed trailhead at the south side of the Cascade Falls parking lot off Mt. Constitution Road in Moran State Park, the well-marked trail to Cascade Falls descends alongside Cascade Creek's ravine. After about a tenth of a mile, look for a short spur trail to the left (east) leading to an overlook of Rustic Falls, where Cascade Creek runs underneath a huge fallen old-growth western red cedar tree before dropping 8 feet over a wide rock ledge, usually divided up into two segments unless heavy flow makes it into one big cascade.

After taking in the impressive view of the modest waterfall, continue south down the main trail along a rough-hewn timber fence that saves hikers from potentially falling into Cascade Creek's gorge. After another tenth of a mile, the trail offers views down to the left (east) of the top of Cascade Falls. At the marked junction with an equestrian/hiker trail, stay straight (south) to continue onto the base of Cascade Falls. Take a left (east) at a small wooden footbridge over Cascade Creek and look left (north) to views of the base of Cascade Falls. Walk upstream (north) along the creek to investigate the lush gorge and grotto around the base of Cascade Falls, where dozens of fallen trees have intermingled with abundant native understory plants in a wild and woolly scene.

It's hard to believe—surrounded by deep, dark, temperate rain forest—that you're only a third of a mile from a road. After indulging in some spray around the base of the falls and having a little lunch or a snack, retrace your steps back over the wooden footbridge and then north up the trail. When you return to the previous trail junction, you can go left on the equestrian/hiker trail to loop back to the trailhead for some fresh woodland views, or choose the hiker-only trail the way you came to get back—either way is about the same short distance back under the evergreen canopy.

Intimate Cascade Falls makes itself at home over a series of large boulders in Moran State Park in the middle of Orcas Island.

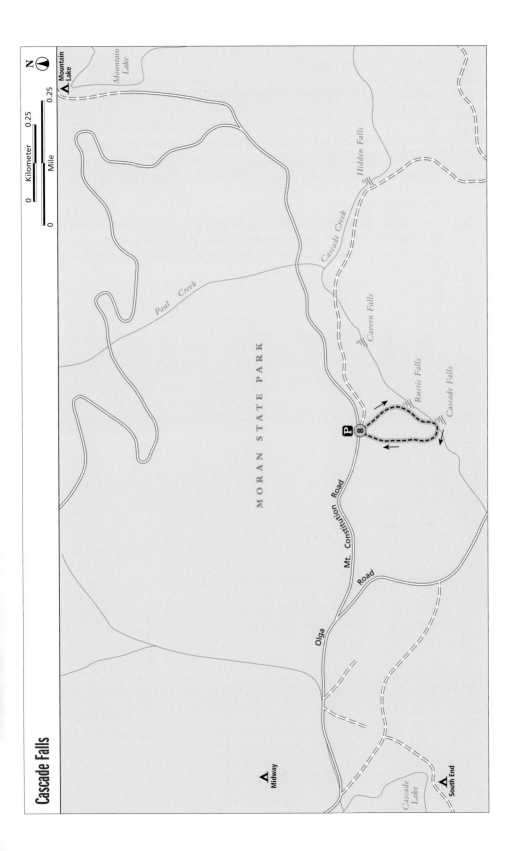

Cascade Falls

Miles and Directions

0.0   From the trailhead at the Cascade Falls parking area (GPS: N48 38.905'/W122 49.961'), follow the marked trail down and to the right.

0.1   Follow a spur trail to the left to see Rustic Falls (GPS: N48 38.853'/W122 49.899'), a small (~10 foot) cataract preceding Cascade Falls on Cascade Stream from an overlook. Return to the main trail and continue south.

0.2   Continue down the trail past some rough-hewn fencing to overlook the top of Cascade Falls (GPS: N48 38.787'/W122 49.937'), then go left (east) at a marked junction with an equestrian/hiker trail.

0.3   Cross a wooden footbridge and walk north to the base of Cascade Falls. Explore the lush gorge around the bottom of the falls. Retrace your steps to the junction with the equestrian/hiker trail, and take it left (west) to loop back up to the trailhead or straight (north) to return via the same route you came.

0.6   Arrive back at the trailhead and parking lot.

9 Whatcom Falls

Whatcom Falls is like an oasis for city dwellers looking for some natural invigoration. The short paved path down to the falls makes it easy for anyone to visit, and plenty of locals flock there on warm summer days to cool off in Whatcom Creek just above the falls.

Start: "Whatcom Falls" sign at trailhead on west side of parking lot where Silver Beach Road terminates. GPS: N48 45.077'/W122 25.742'
Height: 20 feet
Difficulty: Easy
Approximate hiking time: 10 minutes
Distance: 0.2 mile out and back
Trail surface: Paved path to stone footbridge; dirt trail network spreads out beyond Whatcom Falls

County: Whatcom
Land status: Municipal park
Trail contact: City of Bellingham Parks & Recreation Department, Bellingham, WA; www.cob .org/services/recreation/parks-trails; (360) 778-7000
Maps: DeLorme *Washington Atlas & Gazetteer.* Page 15 D10

Finding the trailhead: From I-5, take exit 253 and head east on Lakeway Drive, take a left onto Silver Beach Road and follow it to the parking area near the picnic shelters. The trailhead is marked on the west side of the parking lot. If you parked in the other lot off Electric Avenue, you can walk down via a park trail to the trailhead.

The Hike

Hiking to Whatcom Falls, nestled in the middle of a municipal park on the outskirts of Bellingham, is hardly a wilderness experience, but once you're there nature abounds. Just about anyone can make it down the gravel tenth-of-a-mile path to the impressive stone footbridge overlooking the falls immediately to the north. In fact, during the Great Depression, President Roosevelt's New Deal Works Progress Administration employed local workers to move the Chuckanut sandstone arches from a burned-out building in downtown Bellingham to Whatcom Falls for use in the footbridge, where they still stand today.

Looking south from the bridge is a man-made fish slide that allows newborns from the upstream hatchery to skirt the dangerous falls on their way out of Whatcom Creek. Hikers can continue on via a larger network of dirt hiking trails throughout Whatcom Falls Park. Crossing the footbridge and taking an immediate right takes hikers in only a few hundred more feet to a spot on top of the falls. And farther on, that trail leads to a smaller yet still scenic Upper Falls.

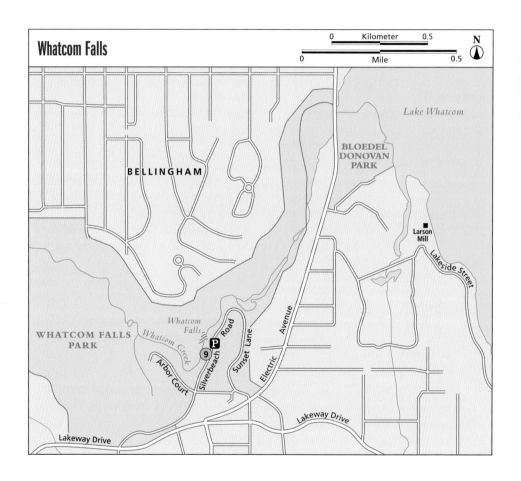

Whatcom Falls is an oasis of serenity in the otherwise bustling city of Bellingham in Northwest Washington.

Miles and Directions

0.0 A sign pointing the way to "Whatcom Falls" (GPS: N48 45.077' / W122 25.742') marks the trailhead off the Silverbeach Road parking lot in Whatcom Falls Park. The wide, paved trail is buffeted by a chain-link fence on the left yielding peekaboo views of the gorge and rushing water below and a stone wall on the right.

0.1 Arrive at massive stone footbridge and cross the middle to take in view of Whatcom Falls to the right (north). Check out the man-made fish slide to the left (south). Return the way you came.

0.2 Arrive back at the trailhead.

10 Racehorse Falls

Remote Racehorse Falls, at the end of a short but challenging unmarked hike, packs a lot of geological punch over the course of its four-stepped 139-foot fall. The two higher sections of the falls sport small punchbowls at their respective bases, while the third forms a fast-moving horsetail of water before finally spreading out wide over a bedrock ledge and terminating in two separate pools.

Start: Unmarked trailhead along south side of North Fork Road about 4.75 miles east of junction with Mosquito Lake Road. GPS: N48 52.977'/W122 07.545'
Height: 139 feet over four sections
Difficulty: Moderate
Approximate hiking time: 30 minutes
Distance: 1 mile out and back

Trail surface: Dirt hiking trail with lots of roots and rocks
County: Whatcom
Land status: National forest
Trail contact: Mt. Baker-Snoqualmie National Forest, Glacier Public Service Center; www.fs .usda.gov/mbs; (360) 599-2714
Maps: DeLorme *Washington Atlas & Gazetteer:* Page 16 2B

Finding the trailhead: Head east on WA 542 (Mt. Baker Scenic Byway) from Bellingham. Some 2.3 miles east of the town of Deming take a right (east) onto Mosquito Lake Road. Just shy of a mile beyond this junction, turn left on North Fork Road after crossing a bridge over the Nooksack River. In 4.25 miles, cross another bridge over Racehorse Creek, then continue another half mile to the top of the hill and park on the right (south) side, just where the road starts to bend left. A turnout where three or four cars could park marks the trailhead (GPS: N48 52.977'/W122 07.545'), which is unmarked but obvious enough.

The Hike

Not the easiest waterfall to access given the lack of trail signage, Racehorse Falls is indeed worth the trip into the heart of the Mt. Baker-Snoqualmie National Forest near Mt. Baker. The trailhead on the south side of North Fork Road appears as a clearing in the trees by a parking turnout but quickly immerses you into second-growth forest primeval, with many scarred stumps from the glory days of logging in the Great Northwest a hundred years ago. Moss- and lichen-festooned Douglas fir, western red cedar, Sitka spruce and hemlock trees dominate the forest canopy in every direction but straight ahead on the narrow and rocky but otherwise well-maintained trail.

After just 800 feet of hiking on a gradual incline, a campsite with a small, improvised rock fire ring and a clearing for one tent emerges on the east side of the trail (for those looking to make a night of it). Continue on another 800 feet or so—luckily the trail flattens out—and look for a side trail branching off to the

Racehorse Falls can prove hard to find but those willing to make the effort are rewarded with a Zen-like scene of serenity.

Even farther off the beaten path, Upper Racehorse Falls is accessed by rope-assisted rappelling down a slippery dirt and rock-covered slope.

right and on down the side of the gorge. This hard-to-see right turn is the way to Racehorse Falls. Sometimes this side trail is marked with blue or pink flagging tied to an occasional tree branch, but don't count on it. From here on in, it's a scramble down the side of a steep gorge, losing 90 feet in elevation over just 300 feet of crumbly, sliding trail.

You'll thank your lucky stars when you get to the bottom safely and behold lovely multitiered, statuesque Racehorse Falls working its way down into a veritable rock garden of car-sized boulders and scary, scattered woody debris. A flash flood in a basin of Racehorse Creek above Racehorse Falls in 2009 created a landslide that cleared a lot of boulders and downed trees from the upper sections of the falls and deposited them around the base, making viewing easier but navigating the terrain below trickier. Fossil hunters might be able to find bird footprints and plant skeletons visible in some of the rocks in the canyon around the base of the falls thanks to the landslide's reshuffling of the geological deck. Wading in the pool at the base of the falls is all the reward you'll need for finding the way, even without trail signs.

Racehorse Falls

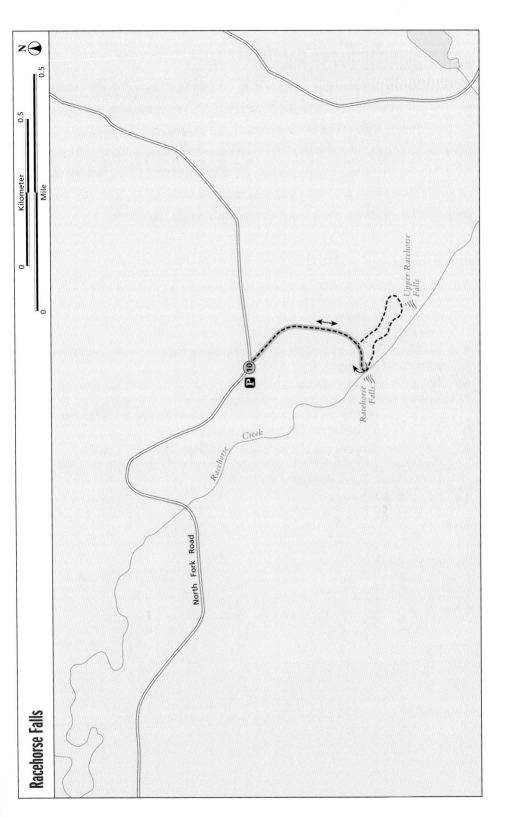

N

Kilometer
0   0.5   0.5

Mile
0   0.5

North Fork Road

Racehorse Creek

P 10

Racehorse Falls

Upper Racehorse Falls

ADVENTURING TO UPPER RACEHORSE FALLS

For an exhilarating side excursion, continue along the main trail another 0.2 mile and look for a side trail to the right (GPS: N48 52.691' / W122 07.338') marked by some pink flagging and some climbing ropes affixed to tree stumps. At your own risk, rappel yourself down the side of the gorge via a series of ropes affixed by previous visitors; beware of rock slides from those above you (best to space yourselves out a bit). At the bottom of a 100 vertical foot rappel you are at the bottom of an upper section of Racehorse Falls, right by a little punchbowl pool perfect for a quick dip—you'll need it after the dusty, sweaty rappel down.

Miles and Directions

0.0 Trailhead (GPS: N48 52.977' / W122 07.545') is unmarked but obvious at around 4.75 miles along right side of North Fork Road as it summits incline and starts to curve to the left (look for a parking turnout by trailhead). Follow the trail into second-growth forest primeval.

0.15 Pass a small backcountry campsite with a small stone fire ring and enough space for one tent to the left of the trail.

0.3 Right before main trail switches back to the left and climbs steeply uphill, look for a small unmarked side trail to the right—there may or may not be blue or pink flagging affixed to some trees marking the way. Follow this side trail down and to the right, and use caution because the dirt underfoot can be slippery wet or dry.

0.5 At the bottom of the side trail, after some steep scrambling—you'll lose 100 feet in elevation over just 300 feet of trail—is the gorge at the foot of Racehorse Falls (GPS: N48 52.760' / W122 07.572'). Return the way you came.

1.0 Arrive back at the trailhead.

11 Heliotrope Falls/Kulshan Falls/ Rock Gnome Falls

Waterfall lovers not scared of backcountry travel will appreciate the short but challenging hike to Heliotrope Falls, a rushing ribbon of water cutting into its own alpine chasm below snowy Heliotrope Ridge on the flanks of Mt. Baker in northwest Washington State. Two other waterfalls on the way up and a view of an icy blue-and-white receding glacier underneath Mt. Baker's imposing peak are a few of the other attractions of the otherworldly trek to Heliotrope Falls.

Start: Trailhead off Glacier Creek Road, 8 miles from junction with WA 542. GPS: N48 48.132'/W121 53.734'
Height: Heliotrope: 400 feet/Kulshan: 150 feet/Rock Gnome: 50 feet
Difficulty: Moderate
Approximate hiking time: 2-3 hours
Distance: 4.6 miles out and back

Trail surface: Dirt with rocks and roots, including three or more stream crossings
County: Whatcom
Land status: National forest
Trail contact: Mt. Baker-Snoqualmie National Forest, Glacier Public Service Center; www.fs .usda.gov/mbs; (360) 599-2714
Maps: DeLorme *Washington Atlas & Gazetteer*: Page 16 5C

Finding the trailhead: Follow Glacier Creek Road south from its junction with WA 542 (0.7 mile east of the town of Glacier) for 8 miles—stay right at all major junctions—to the marked parking area with room for about a dozen cars on the east side of the road. The Heliotrope Ridge trail starts from a kiosk in the middle of the parking area.

The Hike

From the well-marked trailhead, where a trail register beckons hikers to sign in and state whether they expect to come back that day or backpack in, the trail drops down into a typical Pacific Northwest forest, complete with lots of big Douglas fir and hemlock trees and a healthy smattering of boulders, nurse logs, moss, and epiphytes. Within a few hundred feet, the trail crosses a rushing, log-choked stream via a wooden footbridge and then starts ascending, soon passing a sign marking the boundary of the Mt. Baker Wilderness (a protected and roadless area within the Mt. Baker Snoqualmie National Forest).

At about the half-mile mark, you'll pass through an area where the trail gets washed out, as evidenced by the recent-looking installation of a few log boardwalks to pass over the muddiest sections. In another half mile, the real climbing begins as the trail starts going up via a series of six switchbacks in a row before coming upon Rock Gnome Falls, which trickles out of a clifftop above and then spreads out in a sinewy veil over its 50-foot drop.

Kulshan Falls is one of many waterfalls emanating from the glaciers surrounding Mt. Baker's summit.

Wildflowers abound as glacier-fed Heliotrope Falls makes its way down from Heliotrope Ridge near Mt. Baker's summit.

Soon after passing Rock Gnome Falls, the trail begins to flatten out, and in another 0.1 mile reaches Kulshan Creek, a rushing stream that can typically be forded by carefully hopscotching across rocks. A trekking pole (or monopod or tripod) might come in handy to give hikers an extra point of contact on the stream bottom during the crossing. Looking east from the streambed affords views upstream of rolling and tumbling Kulshan Falls, which comes into closer view on the ascent beyond the stream crossing after passing through successive patches of salmonberry and then huckleberry bushes. Mid- to late summer is the best time to hike the trail if berry picking/eating is on your agenda.

In another 0.7 mile of easterly hiking, look for a small, carved wooden sign marking a fork in the trail. Left/straight (east) heads for a crossing of West Fork Heliotrope Creek (if you brought water shoes along, change into them before the crossing, as most hikers end up getting wet up to their knees). Look upstream (south) to Heliotrope Falls as it carves its way down through rock chasms from snow-clad Heliotrope Ridge on Mt. Baker's northern flank.

Then keep going another 0.2 mile—wildflowers are abundant in the summer—to a gorge-side overlook of the dramatic blue-and-white iced Coleman Glacier with Mt. Baker's oh-so-close summit looming above it to the south. The glacier, while still massive, has retreated upwards of 1,500 feet over the last three decades, which is apparent when you look across it to the other side and see the scraped-out canyon wall on the other side, which used to be covered by the glacier.

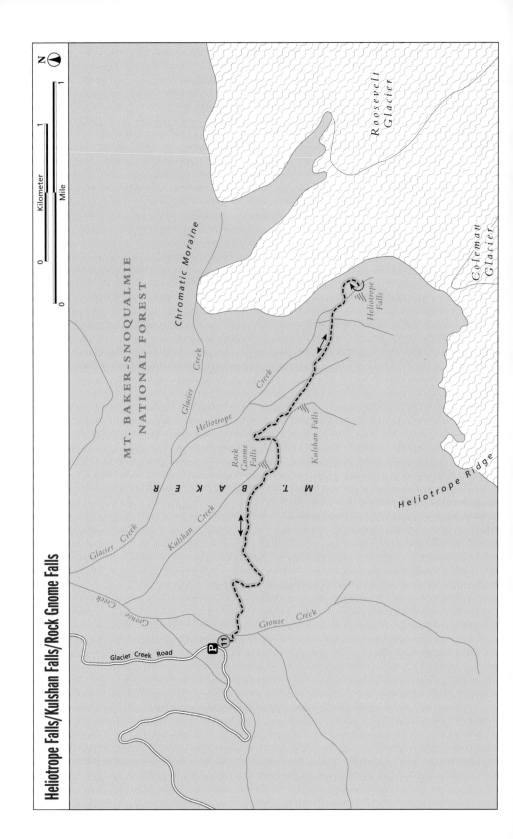

Heliotrope Falls/Kulshan Falls/Rock Gnome Falls

N

Kilometer

Mile

0   1

0   1

MT. BAKER-SNOQUALMIE
NATIONAL FOREST

Roosevelt
Glacier

Coleman
Glacier

Chromatic Moraine

Glacier Creek

Heliotrope Creek

Heliotrope Falls

Kulshan Falls

Rock Gnome Falls

M T.   B A K E R

Kulshan Creek

Glacier Creek

Grouse Creek

Glacier Creek

Grouse Creek

Glacier Creek Road

Heliotrope Ridge

P

11

After taking in the otherworldly alpine view that looks more like Alaska than the Lower 48, turn around and retrace your steps. If time allows, detour on the "Climber's Route" trail, which within 0.3 mile affords alternative views down onto Heliotrope Falls from above and up toward Heliotrope Ridge.

Miles and Directions

0.0 Heliotrope Ridge Trailhead (GPS: N48 48.132'/W121 53.734').

0.5 Cross series of log boardwalks over muddy sections of trail.

1.0 Start up series of six switchbacks.

1.1 Marvel at trickly and veiling Rock Gnome Falls (GPS: N48 47.887'/W121 52.683').

1.6 Cross Kulshan Creek and look east/upstream to view Kulshan Falls (GPS: N48 47.830'/W121 52.411').

2.0 Marked junction of Glacier Overview and Climber's Route trails. (Optional side trip up Climber's Route for access to backpacker's campsite and alternative Heliotrope Falls view adds 0.6 mile to overall hike.)

2.1 Ford West Fork Heliotrope Creek, with views upstream to Heliotrope Falls.

2.3 Arrive at Glacier Overview with views of Coleman Glacier and Mt. Baker. Enjoy the views and then retrace your steps back to the trailhead.

4.6 Return to trailhead.

12 Nooksack Falls

A must-see for anyone traveling along the Mt. Baker Scenic Byway (also known as WA 542), Nooksack Falls divides the North Fork of the Nooksack River into three segments and sends them plunging 88 feet into a grotto-like gorge below. At the bottom, the North Fork continues on to the west but spawns Wells Creek, which heads south. One of the more dramatic waterfalls in the Pacific Northwest—it was even featured in the hunting scene in the movie *The Deer Hunter*—Nooksack Falls is well worth the short detour on a longer trip to the Mt. Baker area.

Start: Signed Nooksack Falls viewing area off Wells Creek Road. GPS: N48 54.344'/W121 48.542'

Height: 88 feet

Difficulty: Easy

Approximate hiking time: 5 minutes

Distance: 400 feet out and back

Trail surface: Dirt trail with lots of tree roots.

County: Whatcom

Land status: National forest

Trail contact: Mt. Baker-Snoqualmie National Forest, Glacier Public Service Center; www.fs.usda.gov/mbs; (360) 599-2714

Maps: DeLorme *Washington Atlas & Gazetteer.* Page 16 5B

Finding the trailhead: Head east on WA 542 (Mt. Baker Scenic Byway) from Bellingham. Seven miles east of the Glacier Public Service Center in Glacier, WA, turn right at the "Nooksack Falls" sign onto Wells Creek Road (also known as FR 33) and proceed for 0.66 mile to the parking area on the left and marked trailhead on right (GPS: N48 54.344'/W121 48.542').

The Hike

Nooksack Falls is not only one of the most scenic waterfalls in the northwest, but is also easy to access. A sign at the trailhead near the parking lot details the history of the falls as a source of hydroelectric power and cautions visitors that at least 11 people have died trying to get better views over the years. From there, a 200-foot walk down a rutted and root-filled dirt trail leads to a clifftop viewing area directly across from the falls proper. A chain link fence protects visitors from falling into the chasm between them and the falls. Another sign warns: "Extreme Danger, Do Not Proceed, Slippery Rocks, No Trespassing."

The falls is named after the Native American tribe that still calls the area home—the Nooksack reservation is based 25 miles to the west in Deming, WA. The name Nooksack either means "mountain men" (as distinguished from Salish tribes inhabiting the coast) or is a reference to the native word for bracken ferns ("noot-sa-ack") that historically served as a staple food item for the tribe.

Kids of all ages will delight in climbing on and around an old-growth western red cedar stump in the middle of the viewing area that sports the springboard scars

Nooksack Falls/Mazama Falls

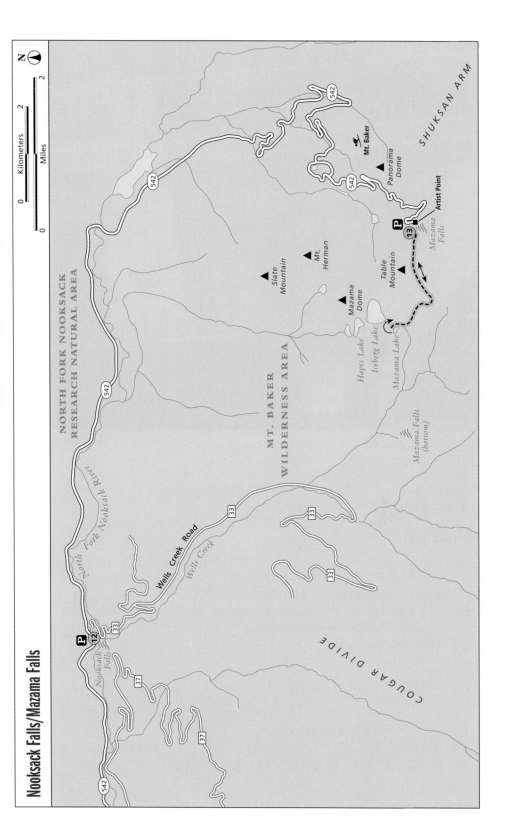

At stunning Nooksack Falls, the North Fork Nooksack River plunges straight down in three segments to join up with Wells Creek some 88 feet below.

showing where loggers of yore would jimmy in boards to stand on while they sawed through huge trees by hand.

Miles and Directions

0.0 A sign pointing the way to "Trail" (GPS: N48 54.344'/W121 48.542') marks the trailhead off the parking area on Wells Creek Road (FR 33). Follow the dirt path down around big second-growth trees and an old-growth stump.

200' Arrive at the falls overlook. A chain-link fence prevents deadly accidents. Return the way you came. (Or explore side trails to the west.)

400' Return to the trailhead.

13 Mazama Falls

Draining the glaciers of Mt. Baker and the Chain Lakes below them, twisting, falling Mazama Falls bounds down 497 feet in four different sections before settling into Wells Creek somewhere near its ultimate base deep in the Mt. Baker Wilderness. Hikers willing to make the short but dramatic hike in from Artist Point at the terminus of WA 542 can spy the top of Mazama Falls' initial 40-foot plunge below Mazama Lake before it disappears from view down its equally steep lower drops, while risk-takers can pick their way down alongside Mazama Falls' entire drop but will struggle with footholds at almost every turn and face quite a return trip back up. Regardless of how much of Mazama Falls you end up seeing, the journey through the Chain Lakes region, one of the Northwest's finest hiking and backpacking destinations, makes it a worthwhile trip.

See map on p. 59.
Start: Chain Lakes Trailhead at Artist Point at terminus of WA 542. GPS: N48 50.801'/W121 41.607'
Height: 497 feet
Difficulty: Moderate
Approximate hiking time: 2-3 hours
Distance: 4 miles out and back

Trail surface: Dirt with rocks and roots
County: Whatcom
Land status: National forest
Trail contact: Mt. Baker-Snoqualmie National Forest, Glacier Public Service Center; www.fs .usda.gov/mbs; (360) 599-2714
Maps: DeLorme *Washington Atlas & Gazetteer.* Page 17 6B

Finding the trailhead: Follow WA 542 east to its terminus at Artist Point, and look for the Chain Lakes trailhead on the northwest corner of the parking lot.

The Hike

Starting out from the Chain Lakes trailhead at the northwest corner of the Artist Point parking lot at the end of WA 542, the trail immediately crosses over a snow bank (which often has a hollow cave inside during summer—be sure to climb inside and look around) and channels you into the thick of a dramatic subalpine landscape complete with stunted growth evergreen trees clinging to rock-studded ledges. Wildflowers and edible berries dot the sides of the trail. Already you'll think you have died and gone to heaven, but push on as the really scenic stuff lies ahead. Within a quarter mile you'll be skirting the flanks of Table Mountain as the trail bisects a steep talus slope with Mt. Baker straight ahead to the west.

While most of the slope is devoid of trees, the trail crosses through a little oasis-like grove halfway across with a carved wooden sign marking the beginning of the Mt. Baker Wilderness, a roadless area off-limits to logging and other development within the Mt. Baker-Snoqualmie National Forest. From there, the trail continues for almost a half mile across the rest of the talus slope and then delivers you to a junction with the Ptarmigan Ridge trail, which leads climbers to the summit of Mt. Baker. Save that way for another hike (or check it out on the way back if you have time), and turn right (north) at the fork to stay on the Chain Lakes Trail, which swings around to the southwest side of Table Mountain and within another half mile offers views into the welcoming green Mazama Lakes basin, where two lakes sit side-by-side and funnel glacial snowmelt into Mazama Falls below.

Streams, rivulets, and snowmelt trickle down across the trail, slippery in some spots, to feed Mazama Lakes. Then pass through a huge boulder/talus field and begin the descent down to Mazama Lakes. Within a quarter mile of the junction with the Ptarmigan Ridge Trail, follow a side trail to the left (southwest) at a carved wooden sign pointing toward "Mazama Camps."

Follow the trail down 100 feet or so and then go left (south) at the next fork toward the camp sites, and then down another 300 feet and straight (south) at the next junction to get out to a rocky perch above the modest creek that becomes 497-foot Mazama Falls' starting point below you. Linger and enjoy the view from the top as the falls spill down a rocky wildflower-strewn ravine and over a downstream cliff face some 40 feet below.

Mazama Falls continues down over three additional sections before bottoming out about a third of a mile downstream. Brave souls can extend the hike in terms of distance and danger by hugging the rocky shoreline of Mazama Falls and follow the falls down for much of its path, but be careful on the slippery, slide-prone rocks that line both sides of the falls all the way down its twisting, vertiginous route.

If you are hoping to spend the night by Mazama Lakes (and are prepared with tent, sleeping bag, food, and a camp stove—no open fires allowed), retrace your steps 100 feet to the previous junction and then turn left (west) to pick a camp site. If none are available, head north on the trail that bisects Mazama Lakes up to Iceberg Lake, where there are two more camp sites, and onto Hayes Lakes beyond that with

ANOTHER VIEW OF MAZAMA FALLS

To get another and perhaps more complete view of Mazama Falls, drive for about 5 miles on Wells Creek Road (FR 33) beyond the Nooksack Falls parking area until it crosses over Wells Creek. The road then starts to get especially rutted and overtaken by brush, but as it rises look upstream to the east across the valley to Mazama Falls. And while the falls are more than 2 miles away from this vantage point, the distance allows you to see all four major sections of the massive 497-foot cascade. On the drive back, keep an eye out for Wells Creek Falls, a 91-foot plunge that drops into a mossy gorge on the west side of Wells Creek Road less than a half mile from the Bar Creek crossing.

Monkeyflowers and dozens of other wildflower species drape the landscape around Mazama Falls during summer.

Mazama Falls drains the glorious Chain Lakes on the flanks of Mt. Baker.

Crossing the ridge under Table Mountain en route to Mazama Falls on the Chain Lakes Trail

a couple more spots for tents. Whether or not you plan to camp up there, it's worth poking around as the alpine lake scenery is beyond beautiful.

When you're ready to return to the car, retrace your steps the 2+ miles back to the trailhead at Artist Point. Yet another option would be to leave one car at Austin Pass down below and another at Artist Point (if your group has more than one car up there) and then do the hike as a one-way, downhill-only through-hike. However you slice it, the Chain Lakes Trail is one of the best hikes in Washington.

Miles and Directions

0.0   Chain Lakes trailhead (GPS: N48 50.801'/W121 41.607') at northwest corner of Artist Point Trailhead.

0.6   Enter into the Mt. Baker Wilderness (GPS: N48 50.790'/W121 42.353').

1.0   Go right (north) to stay on the Chain Lakes Trail at the junction with Ptarmigan Ridge Trail.

1.5   Mazama Lakes come into view to the northwest.

1.75 Follow the carved wooden sign pointing the way toward "Mazama Camps" and turn left (southwest) at the junction toward Mazama Lakes, then turn left (south) at the next junction 100 feet down the trail.

1.8   At the next junction, stay straight and head south to the overlook of the top of Mazama Falls. After enjoying the view down into the falls, wander back toward the camp sites and then follow Wells Creek farther upstream to Iceberg Lake and above that Hayes Lake. Retrace your steps back to the trailhead at Artist Point.

4.0   Return back to Chain Lakes trailhead at Artist Point.

14 Laplash Falls

At Laplash Falls, Bear Creek splits into two channels and then converges over a wide rock wall before dropping like a curtain 47 feet into a rock grotto and disappearing downstream into the lush second-growth forest. The wild and green environment at the bottom of this little-known falls feels like deep wilderness even though the hike in from the road is less than a mile.

Start: Unmarked logging road branching off Baker Lake Road 9.75 miles north of junction with WA 20. GPS: N48 37.283'/W121 44.826'

Height: 47 feet
Difficulty: Easy/Moderate
Approximate hiking time: 1 hour
Distance: 1.4 miles out and back

Trail surface: Overgrown logging road and dirt trail
County: Skagit
Land status: National forest
Trail contact: Mt. Baker-Snoqualmie National Forest, Mt. Baker Ranger District; (360) 856-5700
Maps: DeLorme *Washington Atlas & Gazetteer*: Page 17 E6

Finding the trailhead: Follow the Baker Lake Road about 9.75 miles north from its junction with WA 20 at the town of Birdsview Siding, cross the bridge over Bear Creek, and park at the turn-off for the second dirt road branching off to the right (east), which serves as the unmarked trailhead for accessing Laplash Falls.

The Hike

The hike to Laplash Falls follows an old logging road into typical Pacific Northwest second-growth forest, passing by a couple of "cowboy" (unofficial) campsites. Over the course of its first half mile, the road deteriorates and leads down to a meadow where it becomes a foot trail and then crosses over a rickety footbridge over Bear Creek before winding down into a rock grotto chiseled out by the falling water of Laplash Falls, which looks like a curtain wall veiling down over its 47-foot drop. From the bottom of the falls, the trail winds up and around to a defunct 15-foot tall concrete dam, which feeds the top of the falls. Pick your way back to the main trail and make your way back to the trailhead. The lush underbrush along the second half of the hike makes route finding a challenge, but the increasingly louder sound of rushing water leads the way.

Laplash Falls

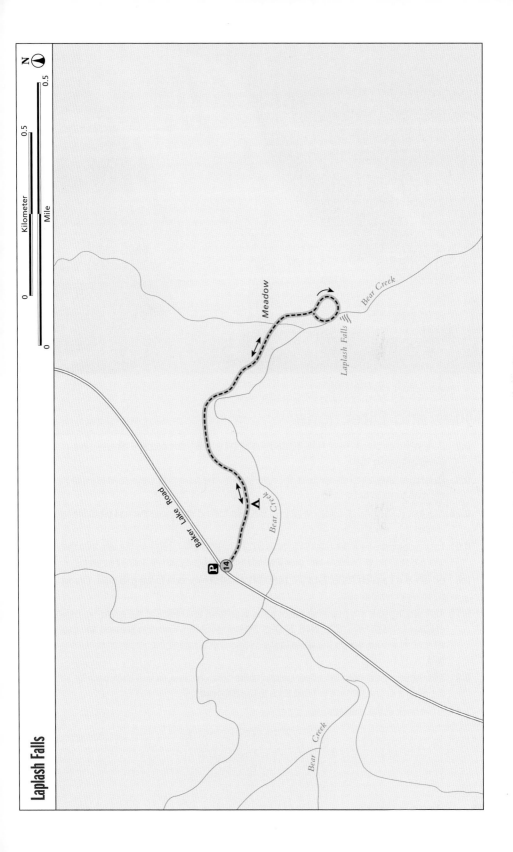

Meadow

Laplash Falls

Bear Creek

Baker Lake Road

Bear Creek

Bear Creek

P 14

N

Kilometer

Mile

0   0.5

0   0.5

The curtain wall of Laplash Falls

Miles and Directions

0.0 Park at the trailhead (GPS: N48 37.283'/W121 44.826') and proceed along an old overgrown paved road.

0.1 Passing an unmarked campsite to the right (south), the pavement starts to erode and the old road turns to dirt.

0.25 At a fork (GPS: N48 37.309'/W121 44.570') in the old road, take the trail off to the right (east).

0.5 Pass a campsite with fire ring (GPS: N48 37.219'/W121 44.290') on the left, then the trail passes into a meadow and over a wooden footbridge spanning a small stream.

0.6 Go left at a junction (GPS: N48 37.146'/W121 44.224'), then follow trail down through 6-foot-high underbrush.

0.75 After picking your way down the twisting and overgrown trail, arrive at the grotto-like base of Lower Laplash Falls (GPS: N48 37.095'/W121 44.245'). Enjoy the solitude and then start working your way up the gorge to the middle and eventually upper sections of the falls.

0.8 After exploring the dam-like upper section of the falls, continue up and hook back up with the main trail and turn left to head back to the trailhead.

1.4 Arrive back at the trailhead.

15 Gorge Creek Falls

Gorge Creek Falls, dropping 242 feet over five distinct sections, is not only one of the most dramatic waterfalls in the North Cascades but also one of the easiest to see, given its location right near a bridge along WA 20 spanning its eponymous gorge. Viewers can park across WA 20 and cross the street to walk across the bridge and peer down into the gorge and the school bus–size boulders festooning the aqua-blue pool at the base of each section of the falls. Like so many scenes throughout Washington's Cascades, Gorge Creek Falls is both beautiful and severe, and reminds us that nature can be both inspirational and perilous at the same time.

Start: Gorge Creek Overlook parking lot on south side of WA 20 east of Newhalem. GPS: N48 41.999'/W121 12.602'
Height: 242 feet
Difficulty: Easy/Roadside
Approximate hiking time: 5 minutes
Distance: 0.2 mile

Trail surface: Pedestrian walkway/grate
County: Whatcom
Land status: City of Seattle (Seattle City Light)
Trail contact: Seattle City Light; www.seattle .gov/light; (206) 684-3000
Maps: DeLorme *Washington Atlas & Gazetteer.* Page 18 D1

Finding the trailhead: Park in the Gorge Creek Overlook parking lot on the south side of WA 20, 3 miles east of the town of Newhalem.

The Hike

Park at the Gorge Creek Overlook parking area on the south side of WA 20 east of Newhalem, then cross WA 20 via the crosswalk—be careful as cars come fast in both directions and aren't necessarily on the lookout for pedestrians. Once on the north side of WA 20, proceed east to the pedestrian walkway along the automobile bridge over Gorge Creek, and look left (north) to see Gorge Creek Falls in all of its five-tiered, 242-foot glory as it thunders down sheer granite cliff faces and past rocks the size of school buses. Brace yourself as cars and trucks cross the bridge and rattle the handrails and grate under your feet. Retrace your steps and return to the parking area. Take an optional walk on the paved path on the south side of WA 20, which starts by the privy bathrooms on the south side of the parking lot and affords vertiginous views down into the gorge below.

Miles and Directions

0.0 Park at the marked Gorge Creek Overlook parking area (GPS: N48 41.999'/W121 12.602') on the south side of WA 20 east of Newhalem and then cross WA 20.

0.1 Arrive at grated pedestrian walkway on the north side of WA 20's Gorge Creek Bridge and look left (north) to Gorge Creek Falls.

Gorge Creek Falls drops some 242 feet right near WA 20, with school bus–size rocks punctuating the aqua-blue pools below each of the five main sections.

Gorge Creek Falls/Ladder Creek Falls/Cedar Hollow Falls

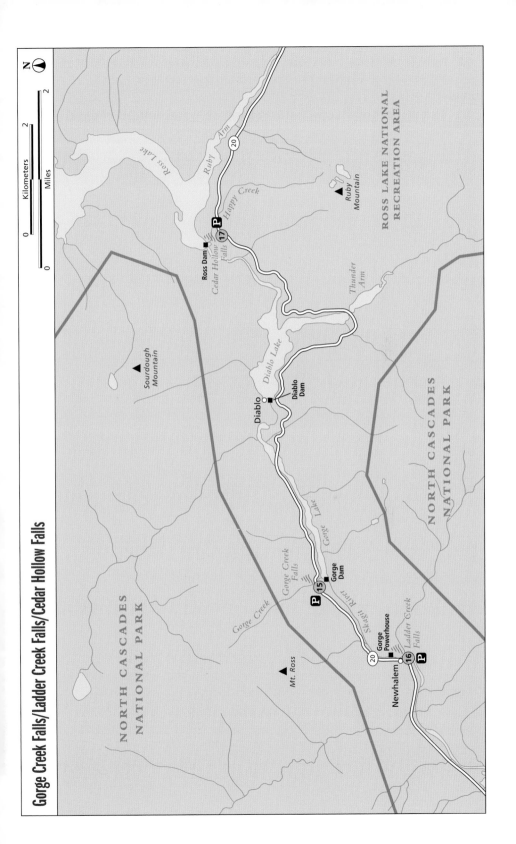

0.2 Return to parking area. Continue south on paved path into gorge on south side of WA 20 and look down at vertiginous views of rock walls and Gorge Lake below.

Option:

0.4 Get to the end of paved Gorge Creek Overlook path and turn around the return to parking lot.

0.6 Arrive back at Gorge Creek Overlook parking area.

16 Ladder Creek Falls

The showpiece for J. D. Ross himself, the man behind the Ross Dam that gives us Ross Lake (a favorite wilderness getaway for Washingtonians), Ladder Creek Falls still sports a multicolored nighttime light display first installed in 1930 to demonstrate how amazing electricity could be. And amazing it is, generating electricity for a large part of Seattle still. But regardless of the lights, Ladder Creek Falls dazzles, dropping 108 feet over three distinct tiers and through a twisting slot canyon of its own carving. Some find the colored lights gaudy, but at least nowadays they feature bulbs that are 90 percent more efficient than the original Depression-era fixtures. Given its beauty, historical significance, and ease of access, Ladder Creek Falls is well worth a stop for anyone driving through the North Cascades on WA 20.

See map on page 71.
Start: Suspension footbridge near Gorge Powerhouse. GPS: N48 40.475'/W121 14.493'
Height: 108 feet
Difficulty: Easy but some sloping trail and stairs
Approximate hiking time: 20 minutes
Distance: 0.5 mile out and back

Trail surface: Dirt trail and some concrete stairs near top
County: Whatcom
Land status: City of Seattle (Seattle City Light)
Trail contact: Seattle City Light; www.seattle.gov/light; (206) 684-3000
Maps: DeLorme *Washington Atlas & Gazetteer*: Page 18 D1

Finding the trailhead: Head east on WA 20 (the North Cascades Highway) to the eastern end of the town of Newhalem. Parking is available in a marked lot (GPS: N48 40.511'/W121 14.532') directly facing the Gorge Powerhouse. Lock up and look for the suspension footbridge to the south (GPS: N48 40.475'/W121 14.493'), which is the beginning of the trail up to see Ladder Creek Falls.

The Hike

Crossing the suspension bridge is in and of itself a trial by fire. Some people don't like the fact that their own (or others') footsteps make the whole bridge react like a giant worm. But 300 feet later it's all over and onward and upward. The trail stops by the Blue Pool, one of the fanciful gardens planted by J. D. Ross that now lies empty, and offers views down into a whirling dervish of a creek below, with giant boulders sending rushing whitewater down like so many pinballs. Then the climb, short but sweet, starts to kick in, with hikers gaining 90 feet in elevation over the next tenth of a mile. A side jaunt midway up to check out the view of the roiling, boiling creek in mid-falls from the vantage point of a classic wooden footbridge perched right over the action is worth the brief detour.

Ladder Creek Falls has carved out quite a path for itself into the green ferny gorge around it.

Back on the main trail, the last 10 feet of elevation to get to views of the horsetail-like Upper Falls are made easier by some concrete stairs, although hikers can take a longer way around via a roundabout hiking path overlooking some of the other now defunct gardens.

Miles and Directions

0.0 Cross the suspension bridge (GPS: N48 40.475'/W121 14.493'), a 300-foot walk over the lower reaches of Ladder Creek.

345' Take the right turn (to the southeast) at the trail junction (GPS: N48 40.547'/W121 14.364') to check out a great view of mid-falls from a classic wooden footbridge (GPS: N48 40.533'/W121 14.343'). Return back to the junction and turn right to keep heading uphill.

0.1 Concrete steps (GPS: N48 40.563'/W121 14.336') get visitors to the tip-top of the viewing area.

The view (with a fisheye lens) from a wooden footbridge over Ladder Creek below the falls

Start the hike to Ladder Creek Falls by crossing the suspension footbridge toward the Gorge Powerhouse.

STILL TRIPPING THE LIGHT FANTASTIC AT LADDER CREEK FALLS

James Ross, that force of nature behind the massive Skagit Hydroelectric Project a century ago, directed the installation of an ornate light show around Ladder Creek Falls in the 1920s and 1930s to showcase the electricity being created at the Gorge Powerhouse below by Seattle City Light. Ross's goal with the show was to create "a paradise of color in the wilderness" and gain greater public appreciation for his still-fledgling hydroelectric venture. For the next 70 years or so, the light show entertained thousands of visitors a year. But over time, antiquated systems and lack of maintenance resources finally caught up with the light show, and Seattle City Light had to shutter it in 2004 due to safety concerns. But public outcry eventually convinced the utility to bring back the light show, and in 2008 work began to restore the system to its former glory—but with a new back end that met current electrical and safety codes. Three years later, the revamped light show opened and has been entertaining passersby and hikers ever since. To check it out for yourself, visit Ladder Creek Falls during the summer any day between dusk and midnight.

0.2   Arrive at the uppermost viewing area (GPS: N48 40.575'/W121 14.339') with view into Upper Falls' slot canyon. A side trail back down meanders through the now-defunct gardens, adding only another tenth of a mile to the total mileage. Or return the way you came via the steps and the main trail.

0.5   Return back to the car at the parking area (GPS: N48 40.511'/W121 14.532') across from the Gorge Powerhouse.

17 Cedar Hollow Falls

Cedar Hollow Falls is a friendly trailside waterfall accessible via a short hike through quintessential North Cascades forest. It makes for a welcome relief from the otherwise deep, dark forest leading down to Ross Dam and Ross Lake Resort.

See map on page 71.
Start: Marked trailhead for Ross Dam Trail at the Ross Dam parking area at mile marker 134 along WA 20 (the North Cascades Highway). GPS: N48 43.667'/W121 03.774'
Height: 126 feet
Difficulty: Easy/Moderate
Approximate hiking time: 20 minutes
Distance: 0.5 mile out and back

Trail surface: Dirt trail with lots of rocks and roots
County: Whatcom
Land status: City of Seattle (Seattle City Light)
Trail contact: Seattle City Light; www.seattle .gov/light/tours/skagit; (206) 684-3000
Maps: DeLorme *Washington Atlas & Gazetteer:* Page 18 D1

Finding the trailhead: At mile marker 134 along WA 20 (the North Cascades Highway), park at the marked Ross Dam parking area and look for the trailhead. GPS: N48 43.667'/W121 03.774'

The Hike

From the Ross Dam parking area at mile marker 134 along WA 20, the Ross Dam Trail disappears into the forest and starts descending quickly through an angled and otherworldly landscape dominated by gnarled trees and huge boulders. The trail curves right and then left and then right again as it zigs and zags its way downhill. After a quarter mile you'll come to a footbridge over Happy Creek. Stop on the bridge and look downstream (north) to see the top of Cedar Hollow Falls hopping and skipping its way down toward Ross Lake. Cross the bridge and continue hiking down the trail to get better view of Cedar Hollow Falls from below. If Cedar Hollow Falls is your destination, turn around and retrace your steps back to the trailhead. Those visiting Ross Dam or Ross Lake Resort can continue hiking down another third of a mile to the Ross Dam Trail's terminus 600 feet in elevation below.

Miles and Directions

0.0 Start at marked trailhead (GPS: N48 43.667'/W121 03.774') on north side of Ross Dam parking area at mile marker 134 along WA 20 (North Cascades Highway).

0.25 Stop at footbridge across Happy Creek and take in views of the top of Cedar Creek Falls, then continue down to see lower views of the 126-foot waterfall. Retrace your steps to the parking lot for an out-and-back hike totaling a half mile. Or continue down on Ross Dam

Happy Creek rambles down a steep pitch choked with rocks and logs at 126-foot Cedar Hollow Falls.

Skymo Creek Falls is one of several waterfalls tumbling out of the forest primeval into the cerulean waters of Ross Lake in North Cascades National Park.

Trail to reach the shoreline of Ross Lake in another half mile (see sidebar) before turning around and heading for the car.

0.5/2 Return to trailhead and parking area.

In Addition

The Waterfalls of Ross Lake

When Ross Dam went up on the Skagit River in 1940 to provide hydroelectric power for fast-growing Seattle, little did planners know what a mecca the resulting 23-mile long reservoir, Ross Lake, would be for nature lovers. Boot paths line the shore and take hikers up above the treeline to peaks made famous by Beat writers Jack Kerouac and Gary Snyder (each served as fire lookouts there during the mid-1950s), while the lake itself provides endless entertainment for fishermen, paddlers, and swimmers.

But if waterfalls are your thing, Ross Lake certainly delivers, with several cascades plunging hundreds of feet off rocky precipices directly into the cerulean waters below. Rent a putt-putt motorboat or kayak or canoe from Ross Lake Resort at the foot of the lake just above Ross Dam and make your way north along the western shoreline.

Five miles up, look for Pierce Creek Falls (GPS: N48 46.199'/W121 04.012') as it chutes through a verdant side canyon and forces its way into the dark and shady shallows. Boaters may have to anchor and walk in to get a closer view of Pierce Creek Falls, which is also accessible to hikers via the extension of the Ross Dam Trail that traces up the west side of the lake.

Another 5 miles up, due west of Ten Mile Island (a great camping spot if you can snag it), Skymo Creek Falls (GPS: N48 51.098'/W121 02.170')—only accessible by boat—gets much more dramatic, horsetailing down some 40 to 60 feet (depending on the level of the lake as a result of drawdown for electricity generation) over two tiers before entering the lake with the force of cannons. Take the putt-putt or kayak in close to get showered.

Three miles to the north, No Name Creek Falls (GPS: N48 53.647'/W121 03.821') follows a similarly vertiginous trajectory into Ross Lake and one more mile farther, Arctic Canyon Falls (GPS: N48 54.121'/W121 04.660') starts out small above the lakeshore but veils out into a wide wall of water into a rock-filled side canyon.

And if you're puttering or paddling around Ross Lake, make sure to save a day for the hike up to Desolation Peak high above the eastern shore, where Jack Kerouac wrote portions of *Dharma Bums* in 1956 while manning a fire lookout cabin there for two months. The hike isn't for the faint of heart: 5 miles up with an elevation gain of 4,500 feet via uncountable switchbacks. But the alpine scenery can't be beat, and if you're lucky you'll get to meet the current lookout who can show you around the tiny cabin that hasn't changed much since it was built in 1932.

Ross Lake Resort, Ross Lake Recreation Area, North Cascades, WA. These classic floating cabins at the foot of Ross Lake near Ross Dam are accessible via a ferry across Diablo Lake and then a flatbed truck ride and then a water taxi across Ross Lake—or you can haul your stuff down a mile through a woodland trail passing Cedar Hollow Falls before picking up the water taxi across to Ross Lake Resort. Call for details on transportation options (keep in mind you will have to haul it back up). Call Ross Lake Resort for an explanation of the options. There is a range of cabin options, some sleep two and others as many as nine ($165–$330/night); open mid-June through October 31. (206) 386-4437, www.rosslakeresort.com. GPS: N48 44.363'/W121 03.682'

Another way to go, especially given how hard it is to snag a spot at Ross Lake Resort, is camping alongside Ross Lake—free first-come, first-served backcountry camping permits are available from the **North Cascades National Park Wilderness Information Center** in Marblemount, WA. Any of the sites will get you into range of the waterfalls via a motorboat or kayak (for rent from Ross Lake Resort). The campsites at Lightening Creek and Cat Island are close to the trailhead for hiking to Desolation Peak. While the camping permits are free, you'll have to get yourselves up Ross Lake somehow, and renting putt-putt motorboats or kayaks from Ross Lake Resort (advance reservations recommended) is the best way to go. (360) 854-7245, www.nps.gov/noca/planyourvisit/permits.htm. GPS: N48 32.198'/W121 26.911'

18 Rainy Lake Falls

Rainy Lake Falls horsetails some 850 feet down steep gray-and-green cliff walls before streaming into the glacial cirque of Rainy Lake. Usually it takes hours or days to hike up into alpine scenery this stunning—some call this region "America's Alps"—but the paved path to Rainy Lake is only a mile from the trailhead off WA 20, making it a popular stopover for those looking to break up the monotony of the long drive through the North Cascades with just a taste of wilderness.

Start: Marked trailhead at south end of Rainy Pass Picnic Area parking lot off WA 20. GPS: N48 30.930'/W120 44.157'
Height: 850 feet total over three drops
Difficulty: Easy
Approximate hiking time: 1 hour
Distance: 2 miles out and back
Trail surface: Paved trail, handicapped accessible

County: Chelan
Land status: National forest
Trail contact: Okanogan-Wenatchee National Forest, Methow Valley Ranger District; www.fs.usda.gov/recarea/okawen/recarea/?recid=59073; (509) 996-4003
Maps: DeLorme *Washington Atlas & Gazetteer*: 18 F5

Finding the trailhead: Park at the Rainy Pass Picnic Area 36 miles east of Newhalem, WA, on WA 20 (the North Cascades Highway) and look for the marked trailhead for "Rainy Lake Trail #310." (Northwest Forest Pass or Forest Service Recreation Pass—$30/year or $5/day—required and available via self-pay station on site.)

The Hike

The paved walking trail to Rainy Lake starts at the south end of the Rainy Pass Picnic Area parking lot and meanders in a southerly direction through deep, dark forest primeval with nary a change in elevation. Pass a turn-off to the right (west) for the Lake Ann Trail—a much more serious hike into the backcountry—and keep straight on the Rainy Lake Trail. At about a third of a mile in, cross a pair of wooden footbridges over Bridge Creek and keep moving south along the trail.

After a seemingly short mile, the trail opens up to an overlook on the north edge of Rainy Lake with views across to its namesake falls. The white torrents of water shooting down the sides of granite rock faces at Rainy Lake Falls look like trickles from this vantage point nearly a half mile away across the lake. But in reality Rainy Lake Falls packs a wallop, dropping some 850 feet across three main drops before skidding over a talus slope and into a verdant gorge before draining into Rainy Lake below. The overlook is about as close as you can get to the falls without doing miles of off-trail bushwhacking, so spend some time relaxing and enjoying the view before retracing your steps back to the trailhead at Rainy Pass Picnic Area.

Horsetailing 850 feet over three main tiers, Rainy Lake Falls feeds snowmelt from on high into the glacial cirque forming Rainy Lake.

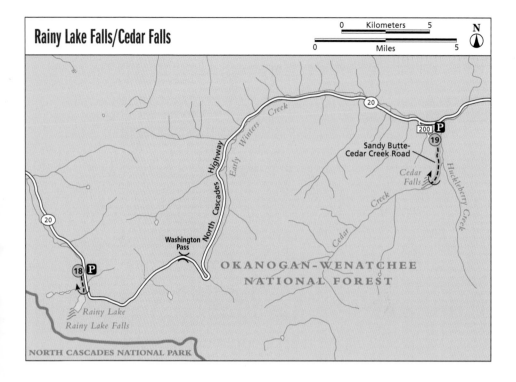

Rainy Lake Falls/Cedar Falls

The Sweet Sound of Engelmann Spruce

One of the trees you'll see lots of on the hike to Rainy Lake and throughout the forests on the east side of the Cascades is the Engelmann spruce. Much smaller and slower growing than its Sitka spruce cousin that prevails in wetter climes like the Olympic Peninsula, the Engelmann spruce is known for its scaly bark and unique four-sided needles. What you may not have realized is that the violin or guitar you play may well contain Engelmann spruce, as instrument makers fancy it for its light, stiff wood. Acoustic guitars made with Engelmann spruce are known for their rich midrange and overall tonal smoothness. Sadly, most instrument makers are finding it harder and harder to find big, knot-free pieces of Engelmann spruce these days, given that the old-growth trees have all been logged out. Luckily we have saved enough of our natural trust so that the Engelmann spruce and other trees we love (maybe too much) can continue to thrive in protected areas like North Cascades National Park.

Miles and Directions

0.0 Start out at "Rainy Lake Trail #310" trailhead (GPS: N48 30.930' / W120 44.157') at south end of Rainy Lake Picnic Area parking lot; pass junction with Lake Ann Trail but stay straight toward Rainy Lake.

0.33 Cross over a couple of wooden footbridges that traverse Bridge Creek as it flows downstream to the east.

1.0 Arrive at Rainy Lake overlook. Enjoy the tranquil scene and wander on dirt trails farther south as desired, then retrace your steps back to the trailhead.

2.0 Return to parking lot at Rainy Pass Picnic Area.

19 Cedar Falls

Mystical Cedar Falls is a welcome sight after a dusty hike through quintessential "eastside" second-growth forest rife with towering pines, wildflowers, and edible berries. The waterworks of Cedar Falls begins upstream as a series of small rapids that then cascade over a 40-foot ledge with a granite knob in the middle before taking a final 55-foot plunge into a dark punchbowl that rarely sees direct sunlight. The animal paths on the cliffs above the falls provide for good vantage points, but use caution as there are no guardrails to save you from a fatal fall into the churning gorge below.

See map on p. 85.
Start: Marked trailhead at south end of Cedar Creek Trail parking area off FR 200. GPS: N48 34.747'/W120 28.719'
Height: 95 feet
Difficulty: Moderate
Approximate hiking time: 2 hours
Distance: 3.5 miles out and back
Trail surface: Dirt trail with lots of rocks and roots

County: Okanogan
Land status: National forest
Trail contact: Okanogan-Wenatchee National Forest, Methow Valley Ranger District; www.fs.usda.gov/recarea/okawen/recarea/?recid=59073; (509) 996-4003
Maps: DeLorme *Washington Atlas & Gazetteer*. 19 8F

Finding the trailhead: Follow WA 20 (also known as the North Cascades Highway) for 48 miles east of Diablo or 4.25 miles west of Mazama and turn south onto Sandy Butte–Cedar Creek Road (FR 200), a gravel road that terminates in a mile at the Cedar Creek Trail parking area and trailhead. The parking area can accommodate upwards of 30 cars and a Northwest Forest Pass or Forest Service Recreation Pass is required ($5/day or $30/year; bring your checkbook to purchase one at the self-serve trailhead kiosk).

The Hike

From the well-marked trailhead at the south end of the large parking area at the terminus of Sandy Butte–Cedar Creek Road (FR 200), start ascending into the classic "eastside" forest characterized by towering ponderosa pine trees, trailside berries, and an abundance of wildflowers. Soon enough you'll hear Cedar Creek, a large tributary of nearby Early Winters Creek, below and to the east of the trail as it thunders downstream but remains out of sight. After about a mile of hiking, all at a gradual incline, Cedar Creek finally comes into view down and to the east of the trail.

Keep hiking for another three-quarters of a mile and just as the trail starts to flatten out, look for an unmarked spur trail to the left (east) that leads down 200 feet to an overlook (GPS: N48 33.503'/W120 28.857') of the upper section of Cedar Falls, where Cedar Creek is divided in two by a huge granite knob and then sent plunging 40 feet down a rock face before regrouping for another 55-foot drop below. Poke

Ponderosa Pines

If you've been anywhere in the forests between the Cascades and the Rockies or down in the Southwest, you've probably noticed the handsome, tall trees with the rust-colored overlapping bark plates punctuated by black crevices that thrive across the region. These ponderosa pines, common along the hike to Cedar Falls, are one of the iconic trees on the eastern slope of the Cascades and on across the rest of Eastern Washington. If you notice a sweet scent in the air next time you're near a few, go in for a closer smell. The tree's resin gives off a scent reminiscent of vanilla or butterscotch.

Besides looking pretty and smelling nice, ponderosa pines are highly sought after for their high-quality lumber, fancied around the world by cabinetmakers and carpenters for finish work. The trees have also proven important to scientists studying historic climate patterns through dendrochronology (tree-ring dating). The width of a ponderosa's rings vary from year-to-year based on how much water was available. With so much going for it, how can you resist hugging a ponderosa pine next time you see one?

The resin underneath the ponderosa pine's overlapping rust-colored bark smells like vanilla.

The 40-foot upper section of Cedar Falls is punctuated by a granite knob separating the cascades into multiple sections before it falls another 55 feet in a lower section.

around in the shallows just upstream from the falls and cool off your feet or more after the dusty hike up.

Then make your way downstream past the falls and pick your way like a mountain goat onto gorge-side trails that overlook Cedar Falls' dramatic 55-foot lower plunge. Make your way back to the junction with the main trail and retrace your steps back to the parking lot, leaving some time to indulge in some huckleberries and salmonberries before returning to civilization.

Miles and Directions

0.0 Start hiking from the marked trailhead (GPS: N48 34.747'/W120 28.719') at south end of the parking area at the terminus of Sandy Butte–Cedar Creek Road (FR 200).

1.0 Look for views through the trees of Cedar Creek downhill and to the east of the trail.

1.75 As the trail finally starts to level off, take the spur trail to the east that leads down to the overlook of Cedar Falls (GPS: N48 33.503'/W120 28.857'). Meander around above and below the raging upper and lower sections of the falls and perhaps enjoy some lunch before retracing your steps back.

3.5 Return to the trailhead and parking area.

Honorable Mentions

F. Colonial Creek Falls, North Cascades National Park, WA

Falling some 2,568 feet from the glacial lake at the toe of the fast-receding Colonial Creek Glacier, high in the North Cascades, Colonial Creek Falls (also known as Hiavaty Falls) is the tallest waterfall on record in the United States, besting North Cascades neighbor Johannesburg Falls by 103 feet and the next tallest, California's Yosemite Falls, by 143 feet. While it's still 2 miles away, the best view of Colonial Creek Falls and its thirteen different drops over half a vertical mile is by looking southwest from the WA 20 bridge over Diablo Lake's Thunder Arm near the Colonial Creek Campground. From Marblemount, WA, drive east on WA 20 for 24 miles and park in the parking area on the west side of the bridge over Thunder Arm. GPS: N48 40.214'/W121 08.426'

G. Jordan Creek Falls, Mt. Baker-Snoqualmie National Forest, WA

This powerful 588-foot waterfall veils down in successively wider torrents on it way to feeding a series of alpine lakes. Hiking the 8 miles out and back (with 2,000 feet in elevation gain on the way there) to see them makes for an exhilarating and exhausting half-day excursion not far from the western entrance to North Cascades National Park. From Marblemount, drive east on the Cascade River Road and in 0.75 mile turn left onto Rockport-Cascade Road. Proceed another 0.75 mile and look for a gated logging road forking off to the left just before you get to the Jordan Creek Bridge. Park there and walk around the gate and up the road for 4 miles. Stay right at the first two forks and left at each of the subsequent two forks and then pick your way through encroaching underbrush to a wall of boulders. Pick your way upstream along Jordan Creek for another 300 feet to the base of the falls. GPS: N48 28.428'/W121 23.154'

H. Depot Creek Falls, North Cascades National Park, WA

This 948-foot juggernaut of a waterfall near the border with British Columbia drains off three large glaciers from nearby Mt. Redoubt, one of the tallest peaks in the North Cascades. Getting to Depot Creek Falls is an epic journey in its own right, requiring a rough-road drive across the Canadian border to Chiliwack Lake to pick up the trailhead that leads to a 3.5-mile hike back across the border into a remote and seldom-visited corner of North Cascades National Park. GPS: N48 58.639'/W121 17.086'

I. Lilian Creek Falls, Ross Lake National Recreation Area, WA

This pretty horsetail waterfall drains Lilian Creek from its glacial source 5,000 feet above, and is viewable right from WA 20. From Newhalem, drive east for 14 miles on WA 20 and look for the falls from a signed bridge over Lilian Creek. GPS: N48 43.283'/W121 01.081'

Eastern Washington

While Seattle and environs west of the Cascade Mountains are famous for their wet weather, the climate just 100 miles to the east in the high desert plateau of the Columbia River basin couldn't be any different. With the brunt of the precipitation coming off Pacific Ocean storms absorbed by the Cascades, Eastern Washington gets much less rain than the western third of the state. The relatively flat topography stretching from the

Eastern Washington's high desert plateau is perfect for wind farms.

Ellensburg region in the middle of the state east into Idaho was formed primarily by ancient lava flows followed by catastrophic ice age floods following the breakup of a massive ice dam near present-day Missoula, Montana. While Eastern Washington may not have the wet weather and vertiginous terrain of other parts of the state, its mighty rivers ensure that the waterfalls that are there, while fewer and farther between, still pack quite a wallop.

Camping and Accommodations

Palouse Falls State Park, LaCrosse, WA: This is *the* place to stay (literally, the only place to stay!) if you are making a pilgrimage to check out the official waterfall of Washington State, Palouse Falls. The 105-acre camping area with eleven tent sites ($12–$31/night) and one pit toilet restroom may seem bare bones, but it is perched at the lip of Palouse Falls' majestic canyon in the high desert of eastern Washington, worlds away from the urban trappings of nearby Spokane and far-off Seattle. First-come, first-served (advance reservations not accepted). (509) 646-9218, www.parks .wa.gov/559/Palouse-Falls. GPS: N46 39.824'/W118 13.676'

Riverside State Park Bowl and Pitcher Area, Spokane, WA: This car camp-ground within 10,000-acre Riverside State Park ($30–$45/night) has sixteen stan-dard tent sites and sixteen hookup-enabled sites for RVs, as well as two group sites for parties of twenty or more. Restrooms (with showers!), water spigots, fire pits, and picnic tables—along with easy access to the river for swimming, paddling, or fishing—complete the deal. More spots are available at nearby Nine Mile Creek Recreation Area as well as at Lake Spokane Campground, both of which are part of the Riverside State Park complex. Open May 15 through September 15. Advance reservations recommended via Washington State Parks website. (509) 465-5064, www .parks.wa.gov/573/Riverside. GPS: N47 41.726'/W117 29.639'

Liberty Lake Regional Park, Liberty Lake, WA: The small but welcoming car campground within the 3,500-acre Liberty Lake Regional Park has nine tent sites, twenty-one RV sites (water and power hookups only), a group camping site, and two "lake view" cabins ($20–$45/night), as well as bathrooms with flush toilets and showers and garbage services. Kids of all ages will enjoy swimming, paddling, or fish-ing right on Liberty Lake, or playing a round of beach volleyball with other campers. Location is ideal for checking out the Washington–Idaho border region, not to men-tion Liberty Lake Falls. Open May 16 through September 15. Advance reservations recommended via the Spokane County Parks, Recreation and Golf. (509) 477-4730, www.spokanecounty.org/parks/content.aspx?c=1868. GPS: N47 37.312'/W117 03.341'

20 Spokane Falls

Walk this loop around picturesque Spokane Falls and get a feel for what makes Eastern Washington's biggest city so special—that is, the intersection of culture (downtown Spokane), industry (hydroelectric power), and natural beauty (a raging waterfall). Less than a mile of walking brings you to two footbridges with waterfall views, not to mention some of the best people-watching east of Seattle. While not necessarily the most scenic waterfall in the state, Spokane Falls is nevertheless a must-see for anyone passing through Spokane.

Start: Parking lot near the corner of West Howard Avenue and North Howard Street. GPS: N47 39.910'/W117 25.131'

Height: 146 feet over several drops; largest drop at Upper Spokane Falls ~90 feet

Difficulty: Easy

Approximate hiking time: 10-20 minutes

Distance: 0.8 mile loop

Trail surface: Paved and handicapped-accessible

County: Spokane

Land status: Municipal park

Trail contact: City of Spokane; https://beta.spokanecity.org/riverfrontpark; (509) 456-4386

Maps: DeLorme *Washington Atlas & Gazetteer*: Page 55 6D

Finding the trailhead: Park in the public lot near the corner of West Mallon Avenue and North Howard Street in downtown Spokane, WA. Walk west toward Riverfront Park and the Spokane River.

The Hike

Park in the public parking lot ($5/day) near the corner of West Mallon Avenue and North Howard Street in downtown Spokane. Walk west toward North Howard Street and the Spokane River and into Riverfront Park. Look for a modern and graceful footbridge down to the left (south), and cross over the Spokane River on it.

Look right (west) for views of frothy Upper Spokane Falls as it shuffles and crashes downstream over a wall of boulders. Stop at Canada Island in the middle of the river and check out a restored 36-foot-tall native totem pole and interpretive displays about the native and industrial histories of the region—and great views of Upper Spokane Falls on both sides.

Crossing over to the south side of the Spokane River, turn right (west)

▶ Huntington Park Natural Area to the west offers better views of Lower Spokane Falls. Another option would be to ride the "SkyRide Over the Falls" gondola over Lower Falls. Up to six passengers can ride in each all-weather, ADA-compliant ski resort–style gondola ($7.50/adults, $5/kids; (509) 625-6601) for the 15-minute ride under the historic Monroe Street Bridge and over Lower Spokane Falls before returning to Riverfront Park.

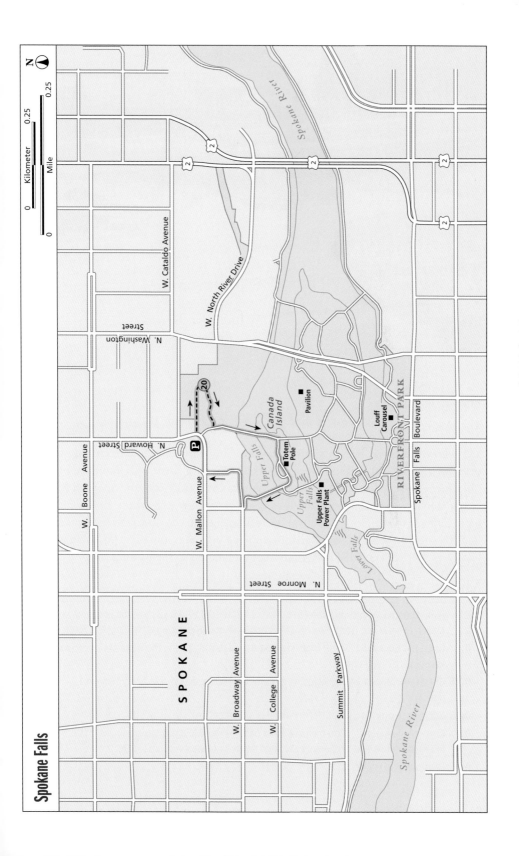

Spokane Falls

SPOKANE

W. Broadway Avenue

W. College Avenue

Summit Parkway

N. Monroe Street

W. Mallon Avenue

W. Boone Avenue

N. Howard Street

Upper Falls

Upper Falls

Totem Pole

Upper Falls Power Plant

Lower Falls

Canada Island

Pavilion

Louff Carousel

RIVERFRONT PARK

Spokane Falls Boulevard

Spokane River

N. Washington Street

W. Cataldo Avenue

W. North River Drive

Spokane River

N

Kilometer

Mile

The Spokane River pounds through the middle of Riverfront Park in downtown Spokane.

and follow the paved trail to another footbridge downstream. Before crossing back over, get a good look at the Upper Falls Power Plant, a classic old powerhouse that still generates electricity for Spokane to this day. Cross back over the Spokane River on the downstream footbridge and look for views of Lower Spokane Falls, which is more difficult to see given the urban encroachments on the downstream riverbanks. Back on the north side of the river, follow the paved trail to the right (east) and work your way over to West Mallon Avenue and continue on to the parking area.

Miles and Directions

0.0 Park in the public parking area (GPS: N47 39.910'/W117 25.131') at the corner of West Mallon Avenue and North Howard Street and walk southwest toward the Spokane River.

0.1 Cross the Spokane River on footbridge to Canada Island; take in the views of Upper Spokane Falls along the way.

0.25 Check out Canada Island, including a 36-foot-tall native totem pole and interpretive displays.

0.33 Cross back over Spokane River on suspension footbridge.

0.5 Turn right (east) and follow the paved trail past the Flour Mill, a historic building now home to several shops and restaurants and onto sidewalk of West Mallon Avenue.

0.8 Return to parking lot.

21 Liberty Lake Falls

Spokane has a lot going for it these days, including a thriving outdoor recreation scene. And while most folks are familiar with the city's namesake falls that plunge alongside a picturesque downtown waterfront, very few are aware of Liberty Lake Falls. A few miles outside of town, Liberty Creek feeds into the popular Liberty Lake, along the way dropping some 30 feet along slides and steps as Liberty Lake Falls. Unlike its thundering downtown counterpart (Spokane Falls), Liberty Lake Falls possesses tranquil beauty. And the hike that leads to it passes beaver dams, an impressive stand of old-growth western red cedar trees, and some inspiring canyon vistas.

Start: Trailhead parking area off Zephyr Road.
GPS: N47 38.116'/W117 03.595'
Height: 30 feet
Difficulty: Easy/Moderate
Approximate hiking time: 2.5–4.5 hours
Distance: 6.6 miles out and back
Trail surface: Hard-packed dirt, duffy, rocky

County: Spokane
Land status: Regional park
Trail contact: Spokane Parks & Recreation; (509) 255-6861
Maps: DeLorme *Washington Atlas & Gazetteer.* Page 55 E9

Finding the trailhead: From Spokane, take I-90 east to exit 296. Turn right onto North Liberty Lake Road. Turn left onto Sprague. After 1.1 miles continue onto Neyland Avenue for 0.8 mile and keep right to stay on Neyland. Turn right onto Lakeside Road and drive 0.7 mile. Turn right onto Zephyr Road and continue 0.3 mile to the park. Follow signs to trailhead parking area. (A $2 day-use fee is required between Memorial Day weekend and Labor Day.) GPS: N47 38.116'/W117 03.595'

The Hike

From the trailhead, follow the signed path that joins up with a gravel road and passes through the campground to a gate. Continue hiking past the gate as the trail makes its way beyond the marshland at the south end of Liberty Lake. At the 0.8-mile mark take a moment to read the interpretive displays that disseminate information about the beaver dams easily seen from the trail.

After 0.9 mile of total hiking, stay straight at a junction and continue along the path now paralleling a gurgling Liberty Creek. The trail climbs gently for the next 1.4 miles, crossing a set of footbridges before arriving at Cedar Grove. The stately stand of old-growth trees marks the end of the easy ascent. There is a warning sign here declaring a lack of trail maintenance and the potential for blowdown (though the path is generally clear up to the falls). Follow the trail across another bridge and begin a steep climb up a set of a dozen or so switchbacks.

Liberty Lake Falls during high flow

The switchbacking ends at the best viewpoint of the hike, looking down at Liberty Lake. The trail now levels off and travels a final 0.7 mile to the falls, occasionally providing eye-widening glimpses across the forested valley.

After 3.3 total miles of hiking, arrive at Liberty Lake Falls. The falls are robust in spring, but reduce considerably in flow as the weather warms. And while there isn't much water passing over the falls by late summer, the splintering cascade tumbles gently over a series of rock steps before a final sliding plunge that make it an attractive and worthy late-season goal.

Miles and Directions

0.0 From the trailhead (GPS: N47 38.116'/W117 03.595') follow the signed path as it joins up with a gravel road that passes through a campground and around a gate.

0.7 Stop to check out an interpretive display about beaver dams. Continue hiking.

0.9 At a trail junction, stay straight.

2.3 Arrive at Cedar Grove. Cross a bridge and continue hiking up a set of switchbacks.

Liberty Lake Falls

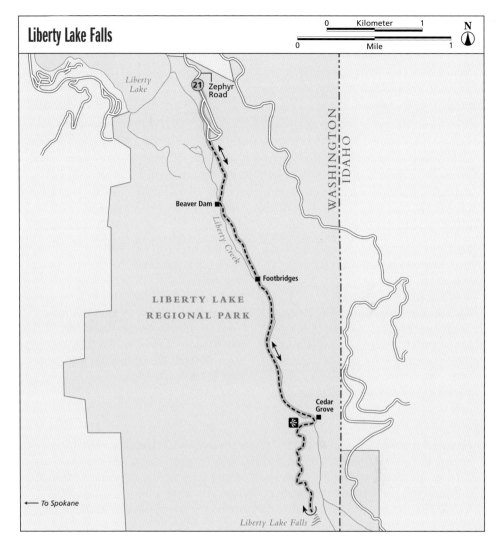

2.6 At the top of the switchbacks, check out the nice view of Liberty Lake.

3.3 Arrive at Liberty Lake Falls. Head back the way you came.

6.6 Return to the trailhead.

22 Palouse Falls

Falling 186 feet into a huge basalt punchbowl canyon below, it's no wonder that dramatic Palouse Falls is Washington State's official state waterfall. While anyone can make it to the paved, handicapped-accessible main overlook across from the falls, hikers can explore a few extended walks nearby as well. Palouse Falls, tucked into Eastern Washington's high desert plateau and with a climate far different from Seattle and environs, may not be on the way to anywhere else, but stopping for an afternoon or camping there overnight is a classic Northwest experience. Pair it with a drive through the rolling, multicolored agricultural fields around the nearby towns of Colfax, Steptoe, and Palouse for a weekend's worth of stunning scenic delights.

Start: Parking lot at dead end of Palouse Falls Road. GPS: N46 39.833'/W118 13.633'
Height: 186 feet
Difficulty: Easy
Approximate hiking time: 10–20 minutes to view Palouse Falls from overlook spots near parking area; 1–2 hours including upstream hike to Squaw Falls and source of Palouse Falls
Distance: 0.4 mile loop/1.8 miles out and back

Trail surface: Paved and handicapped-accessible
County: Franklin
Land status: State park
Trail contact: Palouse Falls State Park; www.parks.wa.gov/559/Palouse-Falls; (509) 646-9218
Maps: DeLorme *Washington Atlas & Gazetteer*: Page 81 D8

Finding the trailhead: Head east on I-90 toward Spokane, and 28 miles east of Ellensburg take exit 137 and merge onto WA 26 East toward Othello/Pullman. Follow WA 26 for 83 miles and then turn right (south) onto WA 261 (Main Street), which goes another 15 miles before a final left onto gravel Palouse Falls Road and another 2.5 miles to a dead end at the parking area (GPS: N46 39.833'/W118 13.633') between the campsites and the falls overlook at Palouse Falls State Park (Discover Pass or $10 day-use fee required).

The Hike

Viewing Palouse Falls couldn't be easier. Park in the parking area where Palouse Falls Road dead-ends and then follow the paved path down to the obvious overlook spot to the east. Meander south along the fence that is the only thing keeping you from falling into Palouse Falls' canyon (keep rambunctious kids close and pets on a leash) and check out different views of the thundering cascade. Work your way south along the fence line to another higher overlook with a roof that offers up views down the canyon from the base of the falls. Then loop back up through the picnic area and campground back to where you started.

Palouse Falls' canyon is an oasis of green in the otherwise dry Eastern Washington high desert plateau.

Marmots live in the rocks on the cliff opposite Palouse Falls.

If you want more, head north from the parking area on a gravel path marked by several log stumps and continue for about a third of a mile, paralleling the railroad tracks for the last bit before turning right (south) on the second dirt path descending into a small side canyon with views directly across to Squaw Falls (also known as Upper Palouse Falls), where the Palouse River drops 20 feet or so as it rumbles across a wide rocky ledge and warms up for the much bigger drop 1,000 feet downstream.

WASHINGTON'S OFFICIAL WATERFALL

Palouse Falls occupies a special place in the hearts of many Washingtonians, as evidenced by the fact that the state's legislature passed a bill (H.B. 2119) in February 2014 designating it as Washington's official state waterfall. The proposal originated with students at nearby Washtucna Elementary School, who petitioned their local representative, Republican Joe Schmick of Colfax, to sponsor the bill. Schmick was happy to oblige and had no trouble getting his fellow legislators behind the idea, especially as Palouse Falls, given its popularity and the parking and camping fees it generates, is one of the few state park sites that doesn't operate at a loss every year.

THE GEOLOGY OF THE PALOUSE

The unique topography of eastern Washington's Palouse region came about during the last ice age when a huge glacial ice dam broke apart around what's now Missoula, Montana, and flooded hundreds of square miles of high desert across the inland Northwest with a sludgy combination of water, ice, rocks, and earth. The Palouse and adjacent sections of modern-day Eastern Washington suffered the brunt of the trauma, and are known to geologists as "channeled scablands" as a result. The scouring of the land eroded out the basalt canyon that forms Palouse Falls and also created the rolling topography of the wider Palouse region. The glacial till left behind from these ice age floods made the area especially fertile for agriculture, and these days Palouse farmers are some of the top wheat producers in the United States.

The trail becomes increasingly rocky and unstable as it continues south into the canyon below Squaw Falls, eventually dead-ending at a rock formation known as Castle Rock that forms the head of Palouse Falls. If you are a risk-taking thrill seeker, pick your way down for views over the top of the 186-foot cascade—watch your step as some rocks are loose and there is no railing to save you from a fatal fall—before retracing your steps back to the parking area.

Miles and Directions

0.0 Park at parking lot (GPS: N46 39.833'/W118 13.633') at dead end of Palouse Falls Road and walk toward overlook.

200' Check out Palouse Falls across the canyon from the fenced overlook, read the interpretive signs there about the geological and human history of the site, and then head south along the fence line for more views.

0.2 Arrive at a more elaborate upper overlook with a roof that features views down into the canyon at the base of Palouse Falls and more interpretive signs.

0.3 Pass through Palouse Falls State Park picnic area and campground.

0.4 Return to the parking area and call it a day, or continue north on the gravel road past the log stumps to hike around to the source of Palouse Falls.

0.75 Take second dirt path to the right (east) down into the canyon formed by Squaw Falls (Upper Palouse Falls).

0.9 Drop down into a basalt canyon and view ~20 foot Squaw Falls (also known as Upper Palouse Falls) directly across the Palouse River.

1.1 Arrive at Castle Rock at the top of Palouse Falls. Retrace your steps back to the parking lot.

1.8 Return to parking lot.

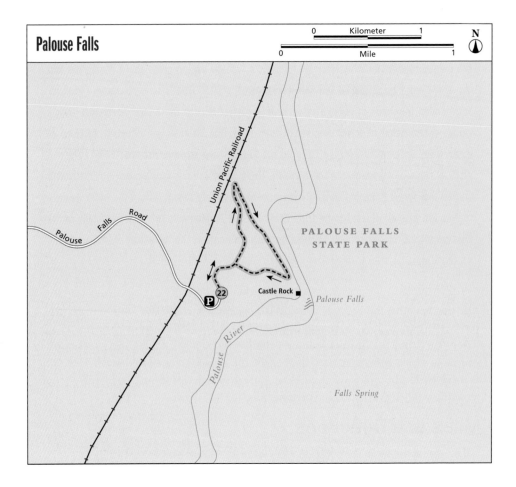

Washington's Waterfall Record

White-water kayakers and adventure sports enthusiasts around the world know Palouse Falls as the site where 22-year-old Tyler Bradt set the world record waterfall descent in a kayak in 2009. Bradt survived unscathed save for a sprained wrist and a broken paddle. His feat, as documented on the pages of *Sports Illustrated*'s May 18, 2009, issue, still stands as the world record to this day.

23 Ancient Lake Falls

Ancient Lake and the watershed that feeds into it constitute a true oasis in the otherwise dry and dusty high desert Columbia plateau outside of George, Washington. After a little hiking, serene Upper Ancient Lake beckons, spawning its own set of waterfalls that in turn feed a meadow that funnels into more dramatic Ancient Lake Falls and its namesake lake below. If you're traveling on I-90 and need to stretch the legs or are camping at the Gorge before/after a concert, the Ancient Lake hike makes for a pleasant half-day excursion.

Start: "Ancient Lake Trail" metal stamped sign at parking area off Quincy Lakes Unit access road. GPS: N47 09.117'/W119 55.358'
Height: 100 feet
Difficulty: Moderate
Approximate hiking time: 1–2 hours
Distance: 2 miles out and back
Trail surface: Dirt trail with some steep rocky sections and stream hopscotching.

County: Grant
Land status: State wildlife refuge
Trail contact: Washington Department of Fish & Wildlife, Columbia Basin Wildlife Area; wdfw .wa.gov/lands/wildlife_areas/columbia_basin; (509) 765-6641
Maps: DeLorme *Washington Atlas & Gazetteer.* Page 64 D2

Finding the trailhead: From I-90 in George, WA, take exit 151 and head north on WA 281 for 5 miles. Turn left (west) on Road 5 NW and follow it for 3 miles before turning left sharply on an unmarked gravel road. Proceed another third of a mile until you reach the parking area on the right. If the gate there is open, you can keep driving and take the next right into another parking area right at the trailhead. If the gate is closed/locked, park at that upper parking lot and hike the third of a mile down to the trailhead, which is marked with a metal stamped "Ancient Lake Trail" sign (GPS: N47 09.117'/W119 55.358'). Either way, parking requires a Discover Pass ($35/year or $11.50/day; wdfw.wa.gov/licensing/discoverpass).

The Hike

From the trailhead at the stamped metal "Ancient Lake Trail" sign, hike on an old Jeep road for 800 feet and go right (north) at the fork and follow the trail as best you can through an oasis-like alder grove that conceals an audible stream and frames the trail in graceful living and dead tree boughs. Cross through the grove and turn left (west) following the line of a ridge and aiming for the power lines that will beckon as you make your way out of the tree cover. Within another 0.2 mile, cross right under the power lines and continue on the road/trail up a ridge heading west. Soon enough a view opens up to the southwest of lovely little Judith Pool, a natural pond that feeds Ancient Lake Falls and Ancient Lake below. The trail starts traversing a ridge and takes you about 100 feet above lovely little Judith Pool. Cool basalt rock formations reflected in typically still Judith Pool, complete with wildflowers and other greenery

Upper Ancient Lake Falls drops in three segments across a wide cliff face.

A stamped metal sign beckons hikers to the Ancient Lake Trail.

in the foreground, make for amazing views and the first of several Kodak moments on this short but rewarding hike.

At a fork, go left (southwest) and down toward a rock outcropping on the edge of a natural dam that contains most of the water in Judith Pond while letting a little bit over to feed Upper Ancient Lake Falls and the watershed below. Keep moving down through some cutouts in the rock and get an up-close-and-personal view on Upper Ancient Lake Falls, which fans out across a 125-foot stretch of rock and divides itself into smaller individual waterfalls when water is scarcer in late summer and fall. The trail passes right next to the northernmost of the three sections of Upper Ancient Lake Falls, a horsetail that froths and bounces its way down 20 feet of nearly vertical rock and showers passing hikers. The other two sections of the falls are bigger and badder, with the third and southernmost one veiling out over five different natural obstacles and falling more than 50 vertical feet overall. Feel free to linger by Upper Ancient Lake Falls, but the bigger show still lies ahead.

Watch your step as you pick your way down the steep and slide-prone hill past Upper Ancient Lake Falls and down into a verdant meadow below. Follow the sounds of the trickling stream, although it might be hard to pinpoint through all the thick underbrush. When you cross over the stream as you head west for the break in the hills that hints at Ancient Lake's proximity, you'll know you're on the right path. In another quarter mile the remnant trail delivers you to the top of Ancient Lake Falls.

Ancient Lake Falls plunges 50 feet to the shores of Ancient Lake below.

Stop to catch your breath and drink in the unique view from above as the stream you just crossed rappels itself down a 50-foot rock wall and then careens into Ancient Lake below.

Venturing down to the lakeshore on scree slopes is an adventure in and of itself—try not to slide on a magic carpet of flinty stones—but well worth the effort to get a better look at Ancient Lake Falls, which starts off with a big drop (~40 feet) that drops into a pool on a rock ledge before widening out and falling another 10 feet through a gorge before finally emptying into azure and oasis-like Ancient Lake. Follow it down to the waterline and enjoy the riparian zone before retracing your steps back to the trailhead.

Miles and Directions

0.0 Pass the stamped metal "Ancient Lake Trail" sign marking the trailhead (GPS: N47 09.117' / W119 55.358').

0.15 Go right (north) at the fork, cross through an alder grove and follow the trail as it turns left (west) following a ridge line toward some power lines.

0.4 Cross under power lines and continue west on road/trail as it traverses a ridge with views of Judith Pool opening up to the southwest.

Ancient Lake Falls

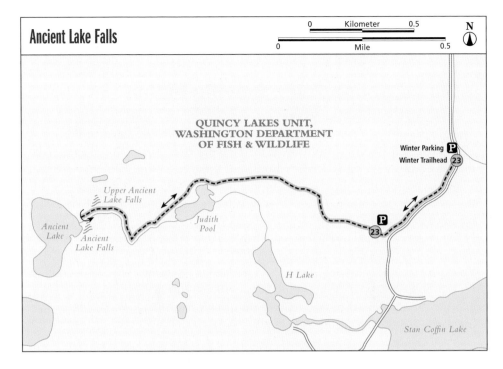

0.6 At a trail junction, choose the left fork (toward the southwest)—finally losing the road—and cut down to an outcropping overlooking the top of the natural dam that forms the western edge of Judith Pool and the top of Upper Ancient Lake Falls.

0.7 From the rock outcropping with views of the natural dam forming the western edge of Judith Pool and the top of Upper Ancient Lake Falls, continue down the steep trail to a verdant meadow below and continue west, crossing the stream in the process.

1.0 Arrive at the top of Ancient Lake Falls. Pick your way down the scree slopes to the base of the falls and the rocky shoreline of Ancient Lake. Enjoy the scene and then retrace your steps back to the trailhead.

2.0 Return to trailhead.

Honorable Mentions

J. Powerhouse Falls, Colville Indian Reservation, WA

The Nespelem River falls 10 and then 55 feet over wide rock ledges at this roaring waterfall on Colville tribal land in the high desert of Eastern Washington. The foundation of an old hydroelectric powerhouse at the base of the falls now serves as a viewing platform for those willing to scamper down the side of the gorge to get the view from the bottom. It's also known as Nespelem Falls and Spray Falls. From the town of Coulee Dam, WA, drive north on WA 155 for 14 miles to the Colville Indian Reservation and turn left onto Columbia River Road (also known as BIA 10), following it for 1.5 miles to a pull-out on the left (south). Park there and walk down a dirt road to the left, staying left at a fork, for about a third of a mile, to the rim of the canyon for a view of the upper half of Powerhouse Falls. A steep, rough trail drops into the canyon from there and leads down quickly to the base of the falls in 500 harrowing feet of hiking. GPS: N48 07.967'/W119 00.395'

K. Drury Falls, Okanogan-Wenatchee National Forest, WA

Anyone driving on US 2 west of Leavenworth probably has spied the 600-foot upper tier of Drury Falls as gravity pulls Fall Creek down the wall of Tumwater Canyon into a verdant chute below. A couple of spots along US 2 yield more views to the falls' middle tier, but the only way to see the full 1,270-foot waterfall—one of the tallest in Washington State—is from the summit of nearby Tumwater Mountain, accessible on foot via a trail network starting at the end of Ranger Road off Leavenworth's Ski Hill Drive. From US 2 in Leavenworth, drive north on Ski Hill Drive for 0.7 mile, then turn left onto Ranger Road and park at its terminus at the eastern end of Tumwater Mountain. Hike west onto the ridge and follow it northwest for 2.5 to 3 miles for the best views of Drury Falls across Tumwater Canyon. GPS: N47 38.213'/W120 44.772'

Central Cascades

Washington's Central Cascades, with hiking trails, alpine lakes, and lots of opportunities to get away from it all, is truly Seattle's playground, with millions of outdoorsy urban dwellers coming to and through Snoqualmie Pass every weekend of the year. Some of the

Oxeye daisies carpet an abandoned orchard in the shadow of the Washington's Central Cascades near Stehekin.

state's most iconic waterfalls are in the Central Cascades; indeed, sliding down the Denny Creek Waterslides on your butt is practically a Northwest rite of passage.

Camping and Accommodations

Denny Creek Campground, Mt. Baker-Snoqualmie National Forest, WA: This popular Forest Service campground has thirty-three RV-accessible car-camping sites ($20–$32/night). Walking distance to trailheads for hikes to Franklin Falls and Keekwulee Falls/Denny Creek Waterslides. Advance reservations recommended. (877) 444-6777, www.fs.usda.gov/recarea/mbs/recreation/recarea/?recid=18032& actid=29. GPS: N47 24.754'/W121 26.557'

Wallace Falls Lodge, Gold Bar, WA: A great place to get pampered after the hike to Wallace Falls, this bed-and-breakfast-style custom-built log lodge has ten guestrooms set on 10 acres adjacent to Wallace Falls State Park. Trails on the property join up with Wallace Falls Trail. (360) 793-8784, www.wallacefallslodge.com. GPS: N47 52.012'/W121 40.920'

Wallace Falls State Park, Gold Bar, WA: Two walk-in tent sites ($12) and five cabins with heat and electricity that sleep five people each ($69/night in summer, $59 in shoulder season, and $45 in winter), easy access to Wallace Falls hike. Hike to Wallace Falls right from your tent or cabin. (360) 793-0420, www.parks.wa.gov/289/Wallace-Falls. GPS: N47 52.049'/W121 40.747'

Salish Lodge, Snoqualmie, WA: This deluxe lodge with eighty-four guestrooms ($199–$859/night) and two restaurants is the nicest hotel for miles around. And the views over the top of Snoqualmie Falls from the guestrooms and common areas—the lodge is basically built right on top—are hard to beat. (800) 272-5274, www.salish lodge.com. GPS: N47 32.526'/W121 50.205'

Treehouse Point, Fall City, WA: Live out your treehouse fantasy without building your own by staying overnight in one of eight treehouses ($255–$355/night) designed and built by treehouse guru Pete Nelson on 4 acres in the foothills of the Cascades. Easy access to Twin Falls, Franklin Falls, Keekwulee Falls, and the Denny Creek Waterslides, among other destinations in the central Cascades. Open year-round, but two-night minimum stay May through October. (425) 441-8087, www .treehousepoint.com. GPS: N47 32.288'/W121 54.623'

24 Keekwulee Falls/Denny Creek Waterslides

This classic Pacific Northwest dayhike leads through old-growth forest to a family-friendly all-natural waterslide section of Denny Creek—where brave kiddos of any age can slide down the smooth granite rock faces propelled by a sheen of rushing snowmelt runoff—and then up to greater heights and overlooks of awe-inspiring Keekwulee Falls as it horsetails down 35 feet before spreading out and dividing itself over a granite knob before finally plunging another 90 feet in one last sheer vertical drop.

Start: Trailhead at north end of Denny Creek parking area of FR 5830. GPS: N47 24.911'/W121 26.606'
Height: Keekwulee Falls: 125 feet
Difficulty: Easy/Moderate
Approximate hiking time: 2-3 hours
Distance: 4.5 miles out and back
Trail surface: Many steep sections and rocks and roots aplenty, but otherwise well graded and maintained

County: King
Land status: National forest
Trail contact: Mt. Baker-Snoqualmie National Forest, Snoqualmie Ranger District; www.fs.usda.gov/mbs; (425) 783-6000
Maps: DeLorme *Washington Atlas & Gazetteer:* Page 61 9A

Finding the trailhead: Heading east on I-90, take exit 47 (Asahel Curtis/Denny Creek) and turn left (north) to cross the highway and then turn right (east) at the "T" and go another 0.25 mile to Denny Creek Road (FR 58). Turn left (north) and drive 2 miles, passing the Denny Creek Campground. Just past the campground, turn left onto FR 5830, pass the Franklin Falls trailhead and cross a bridge over the South Fork Snoqualmie River. Continue another 0.2 mile to the dead-end parking area. A Northwest Forest Pass is required for parking. Look for the signed trailhead (GPS: N47 24.911'/W121 26.606') at the north end of the parking area.

The Hike

Look for the signed trailhead at the north end of the Denny Creek parking area, which can accommodate ~50 cars (with overflow parking available along the road) and has two pit-toilet privies. Follow the trail as it quickly ascends into glorious old-growth temperate rain forest with huge western red cedar, hemlock, and Douglas fir trees dominating the canopy layer. The rushing sounds of Denny Creek to the South Fork Snoqualmie River compete with traffic noise from nearby I-90, which passes over the trail via a huge set of concrete spans some 200 feet above the forest floor.

After a half mile of hiking, the trail crosses directly under I-90. From there the trail starts to ascend more vigorously, crossing into the Alpine Lakes Wilderness, as marked

Keekwulee Falls

Denny Creek Waterslides can be a popular destination on a hot summer day.

by a carved wooden sign nailed to a tree. Keep climbing and check out rolling and tumbling Denny Creek to the west of the trail as it cascades over bumps and dips in a frothy and turbulent trip downstream.

Within another half mile the trail dips down into the gorge around Denny Creek and dumps you at the edge of Denny Creek toward the bottom of the famed waterslides, where the combination of smooth rocks and fast-moving water have been delighting the young at heart for eons. Expect to get wet up to your ankles at least in fording 25-foot-wide Denny Creek (sandals or water shoes, let alone a trekking pole or tripod/monopod, would come in handy). Once safely across to the west side of Denny Creek, spend some time wandering around the upper sections of the waterslides. Take a hydration or lunch break on the broad, flat rocks that serve as veritable bleachers as dozens of onlookers watch kids and other bold souls ride the natural waterslides on their butts.

Once revived and restored, pick up the trail from there and continue west to make the push up to view Keekwulee Falls. Continuing back into the forest, the trail gets steeper and rockier, but the understory wildflowers and ferns provide a nice visual backdrop to the tougher-going. Rushing Denny Creek down to the right (east) is always there to keep you company as you proceed another half mile to a big debris slide where lots of big rocks have piled up, affording your first view across the valley to the northeast of Keekwulee Falls as it drains a snowfield before dodging and weaving over giant granite stair steps before finally freefalling over a ledge and plunging 90 feet in one drop.

Denny Creek funnels into a fast-running chute just above the waterslides.

Keekwulee Falls/Denny Creek Waterslides/Franklin Falls

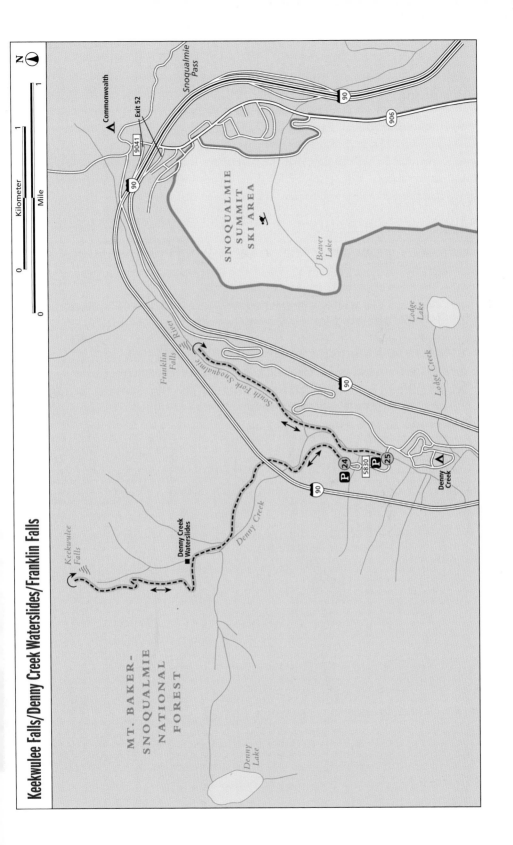

While these full frontal views of the falls are great, push on another 0.2 mile to a junction with a small spur trail to the right (east) that leads down to the snowfield and rocks above Keekwulee Falls. The side trail winds down quickly through dense, stunted alpine trees, leading to a granite shoot with some rocky footholds built in by nature. Squeezing through this last obstacle, you'll find yourself on a big flat expanse of several layered huge granite cliffs that channel the source waters of Denny Creek into Keekwulee Falls and, below that, the waterslides. Watch your step as your explore this dramatic natural wonderland. Then retrace your steps and make your way back down past the waterslides and back to the parking area.

Miles and Directions

0.0   Trailhead (GPS: N47 24.911'/W121 26.606') at north end of Denny Creek parking area off FR 58.

0.5   Trail crosses directly under I-90 spans, 200 feet above.

1.0   Cross into the Alpine Lakes Wilderness (GPS: N47 25.339'/W121 26.947') and start looking for views through the trees to the west for smaller cascades along rushing Denny Creek.

1.5   Arrive at Denny Creek Waterslides (GPS: N47 25.490'/W121 27.109').

2.0   Rock slide crosses trail; view to the northeast of Keekwulee Falls opens up.

2.1   Take the short side trail (GPS: N47 25.887'/W121 27.188') to the right (east) that leads to rock outcroppings above Keekwulee Falls.

2.25 Peer over the top of Keekwulee Falls from its source. Turn around and retrace your steps back to trailhead.

4.5   Return back at trailhead.

25 Franklin Falls

Franklin Falls is a quintessential Pacific Northwest waterfall, with two small upper drops tucked into a woodland ravine followed by a final 70-foot plunge into a roiling pool below. Scattered downed evergreen trees and glacier-strewn boulders complete the scene at the destination end of this short yet invigorating hike. Some decry that I-90 is within view of Franklin Falls, while others delight in this juxtaposition of man and nature. Given its beauty and accessibility, Franklin Falls is one of the most popular waterfall hikes in Washington State.

See map on p. 117.
Start: Trailhead on north side of FR 5830. GPS: N47 24.789' / W121 26.562'
Height: 135 feet broken up into three sections, with only lower 70-foot section visible from end of main trail
Difficulty: Moderate
Approximate hiking time: 2 hours
Distance: 2 miles out and back

Trail surface: Rocky trail, some wooden footbridges
County: King
Land status: National forest
Trail contact: Mt. Baker-Snoqualmie National Forest, Snoqualmie Ranger District; www.fs .usda.gov/mbs; (425) 783-6000
Maps: DeLorme *Washington Atlas & Gazetteer:* Page 61 9A

Finding the trailhead: Heading east on I-90, take exit 47 (Asahel Curtis/Denny Creek) and turn left (north) to cross the highway and then turn right (east) at the "T" and go another 0.25 mile to Denny Creek Road (FR 58). Turn left (north) and drive 3 miles, passing the Denny Creek Campground. Just past the campground, turn left onto FR 5830 and park before crossing the bridge. Look for a sign marking the trailhead (GPS: N47 24.789' / W121 26.562') on the north side of the road.

The Hike

The hike to Franklin Falls starts out gently on an often muddy trail that leads down to some smooth boulders at the edge of the South Fork Snoqualmie River. Stop for a picture and to rinse your hands in the cold rushing water, then keep moving. Old rustic vacation cabins peek in and out of view from the surrounding forest. Then the trail starts to climb via a series of log stair-steps; similarly rough-hewn guardrails warn against peering over the increasingly steep edge. After this modest elevation gain, the trail levels off, yielding even more dramatic bird's-eye views down to the fast-moving South Fork Snoqualmie, now a hundred feet or so below.

The trail has a junction at one point with FR 58, a dirt road that climbs up separately from the Denny Creek Campground. Eventually a carved wooden sign at a fork points the way down to Franklin Falls. A quick descent gets hikers to the edge of the pool at the base of the falls. Be careful exploring the rocks and logs nearing the base of the falls, as they are slippery year-round thanks to the abundant spray.

Franklin Falls is a popular destination on warm summer days.

Those craving more views of falling water can access the upper two drops of Franklin Falls, not visible from the hiking trail or from the base of the falls, north of I-90. The uppermost drop is 15 feet and the secondary one is 25 feet before the falls turn right via a 25-foot slide before plunging the final 70 feet visible from the base to its roiling pool below.

Canyoneering aficionados will find lots to do in and around these two upper tiers. To experience them, drive (or hike) up FR 58 for 2 miles beyond the Denny Creek Campground to a large pull-out on the left side of the road, where an unmarked but obvious 200-foot trail leads to the river and upper falls. While these dirt roads and trails may seem forlorn these days, it's amusing to think that in the late 19th century they were bustling with activity as a key link in the wagon road network traversing what was then uncharted Native lands.

Miles and Directions

0.0 From the marked sign at the trailhead (GPS: N47 24.789'/W121 26.562') pointing the way to Franklin Falls, hike north along the east side of the South Fork Snoqualmie River. Within 300 feet the trail passes a section of river-smoothened boulders.

0.1 The trail passes by several small seasonal vacation cabins.

0.3 A footbridge takes the trail over a particularly muddy and washed-out stretch followed by a series of log stair steps gaining elevation quickly. Rough-hewn timber guardrails keep hikers from falling down the steep cliff into the rushing river a hundred feet or so down below. A huge 200+-foot-tall old-growth western red cedar tree beckons to be hugged, but you'll need several pairs of arms to get around it.

0.4 Look north through trees for view of small double falls along the South Fork Snoqualmie River.

0.5 A small spur turns out to FR 58, which continues up from near the trailhead.

0.8 At a trail junction a carved wooden sign points hikers bound for Franklin Falls to take the left fork. Descend down this trail for ~120 feet and move north toward the falls.

1.0 Arrive at the base of Franklin Falls (GPS: N47 25.500'/W121 26.009'). Return the way you came.

2.0 Return back at the trailhead.

26 Twin Falls

Twin Falls might be the most popular waterfall hike in Washington State given its proximity to Seattle—but don't let that deter you. The mile-long hike in takes you through a verdant temperate rain-forest gorge where fire-scarred old-growth Douglas fir trees and school bus–size glacial erratic boulders compete for your attention before the views start opening up of Twin Falls in all of its multitiered glory as it cuts through a gorge in the South Fork Snoqualmie River.

Start: Trailhead at parking lot at dead end of SE 159th Street in Olallie State Park. GPS: N47 27.157' / W121 42.328'
Height: 230 feet
Difficulty: Easy/Moderate
Approximate hiking time: 1 hour
Distance: 2.2 miles out and back

Trail surface: Well-maintained gravel and dirt
County: King
Land status: State park
Trail contact: Olallie State Park, Washington State Parks
Maps: DeLorme *Washington Atlas & Gazetteer*. Page 61 6A

Finding the trailhead: Drive east on I-90 to exit 34 (Edgewick Road) and turn right (south) on 468th Avenue SE. Proceed for a half mile then turn left (east) on SE 159th Street, which dead-ends at the Twin Falls parking area and trailhead (GPS: N47 27.157' / W121 42.328') in another half mile. (Discover Pass–$5/day or $30/year, available on site–required for parking.)

The Hike

Start out from the marked trailhead on the east side of the Twin Falls parking area where SE 159th Street dead-ends and head southeast on the trail into the forest, with views of the rushing South Fork Snoqualmie River through the trees to the right (west). After a third of a mile look for a short, unmarked spur trail to the right (west) that leads down to a placid stretch of the river—a great place to take a dip on a hot day. Back on the main trail, keep heading south, passing huge glacial erratic boulders and fire-scarred old growth Douglas fir trees. Zig-zag up a pair of switchbacks and stop at a man-made bench on a natural shelf with views east into the gorge and the lower, tallest section of Twin Falls, which free-falls 135 feet from an upper ledge into a small turbulent pool below. Steel up for the upcoming switchbacks with a bite of food and a sip of water before continuing east on the trail.

In another 0.1 mile, pass a fire-scarred but otherwise thriving old-growth Douglas fir tree surrounded by a rough-hewn timber fence. A carved wood sign affixed to the fence reads, "Help us protect this old-growth fir tree by not walking on its root system—soil compaction can kill it." After checking out the tree, keep moving and go right (south) at a junction with some wooden stairs that descend down into the

Twin Falls

Twin Falls

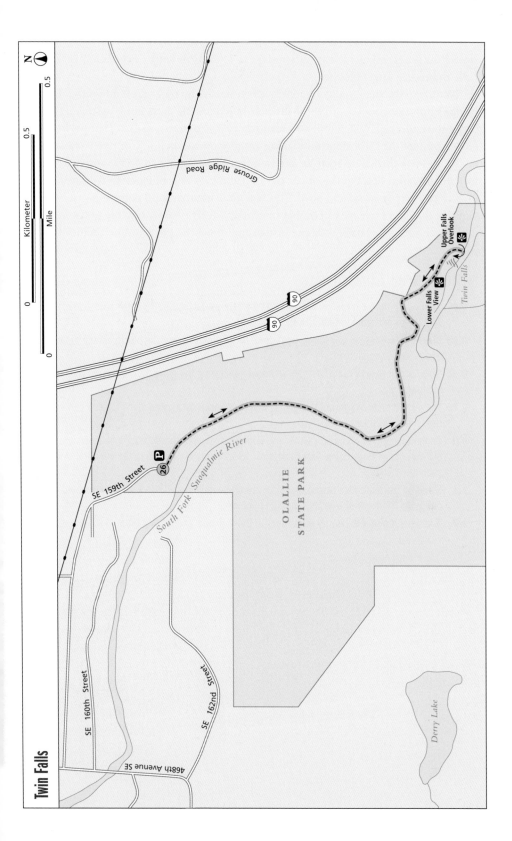

Twin Falls

N

Kilometer
0   0.5   0.5

Mile
0

SE 159th Street

P
26

South Fork Snoqualmie River

SE 160th Street

SE 162nd Street

468th Avenue SE

Grouse Ridge Road

90
90

OLALLIE
STATE PARK

Lower Falls
View

Upper Falls
Overlook

Twin Falls

Derry Lake

side of the gorge below via two dozen steps to a platform with a closer view of Twin Falls' impressive lower plunge.

Return to the main trail and continue southeast. The trail winds down to a footbridge across the gorge over Twin Falls' two-tiered middle drop. Look upstream (east) to see the upper tier, which drops 30 feet over two steps into a narrow channel before crossing under the footbridge and falling another 20 feet below. Continue across the bridge and switchback up again to another bench and then push on for another ~200 feet and look for views of the upper tier of Twin Falls as it plunges 45 feet over two drops into a serene woodland bowl. This is as good a turnaround point as any—better views of the upper tier are impossible since it's partially obscured by the gorge below it. Retrace your steps back over the bridge and down the gorge to the trailhead and parking area.

Miles and Directions

0.0 Start hiking from the trailhead (GPS: N47 27.157'/W121 42.328') at the east side of the Twin Falls parking lot in Olallie State Park.

0.33 Short unmarked spur trail heads west down to swimming hole along placid stretch of the South Fork Snoqualmie River.

0.66 Stop for first view of Twin Falls' 135-foot lower plunge up the gorge from a natural shelf in the forest.

0.75 Marvel at a huge old-growth Douglas fir tree surrounded by a cattle fence to keep curious hikers at a distance.

0.9 Go right (south) at a junction with some wooden stairs that descend 0.1 mile down into the side of the gorge below Twin Falls' lower 135-foot plunge. Return to the main trail and continue southeast.

1.1 Stand on the footbridge across the gorge over the middle tier of Twin Falls. Spy the partially obscured upper tier of Twin Falls through the trees.

2.2 Turn around and retrace your steps back to the trailhead and parking area.

27 Snoqualmie Falls

Snoqualmie Falls, just off I-90 thirty miles east of Seattle, is one of the most popular tourist stops—and probably the most famous waterfall—in all of Washington State. Some 1.5 million visitors a year check out the landmark cascade as it falls off a wide ledge just below the stately Salish Lodge and plunges 268 feet into a large punchbowl gorge below. Beyond scenic views, Snoqualmie Falls also produces 54 megawatts of electricity for Seattle and environs, making it one of the most practical tourist attractions around.

Start: Snoqualmie Falls parking area on east side of WA 202. GPS: N47 32.564'/W121 50.141'
Height: 268 feet
Difficulty: Easy
Approximate hiking time: 10 minutes/1 hour
Distance: 0.4 mile to upper viewing platforms, out and back; or 2 miles adding in trip down to viewing platform across from the bottom of the falls, out and back

Trail surface: Paved; gravel, dirt
County: King
Land status: Private land (Puget Sound Energy)
Trail contact: Puget Sound Energy; www.pse .com; (888) 225-5773
Maps: DeLorme *Washington Atlas & Gazetteer:* 46 E5

Finding the trailhead: Take I-90 East to exit 25 and turn left (north) at the end of the exit ramp onto WA 18 (SE Snoqualmie Parkway), which goes north and then winds around to the east. In 3.7 miles, turn left (north) onto Railroad Ave. SE (WA 202), and look for the signed turn-off to the right (east) for the Snoqualmie Falls parking lot (GPS: N47 32.564'/W121 50.141') in less than a mile. Park and then cross over WA 202 on the covered footbridge to Snoqualmie Falls Park adjacent to the Salish Lodge.

The Hike

Park in the free visitor parking lot on the east side of WA 202 across from the Salish Lodge and then walk (west) over the covered footbridge to Snoqualmie Falls Park. Head straight down to the fenced overlook of Snoqualmie Falls. With the Salish Lodge immediately to your left, enjoy this closest view you will get to the top of the falls, and then walk right (north) along the railing and down some concrete stairs for different perspectives on the thundering cataract. Within a tenth of a mile, reach a platform with a direct view across to Snoqualmie Falls.

Get out your camera and snap a few shots, then continue on down to a second overlook 300 feet farther down the paved walkway. If you're lucky and the conditions are right, you may see a rainbow somewhere near the falls. If the short walk to these upper overlooks is all you need, retrace your steps and head back to the car.

THE POWER OF SNOQUALMIE FALLS

According to the Snoqualmie Tribe, whose people have lived in and around Washington's Central Cascades for thousands of years, Snoqualmie Falls is a sacred and powerful place and is key to their culture, beliefs, and spirituality. "That's where Heaven and Earth meet," says Ernie Barr, Jr., son of late Snoqualmie Head Chief Ernie Barr. "And the mists ... that roll up to Heaven carry our prayers and our hopes and our dreams to the Creator of us all."

But Snoqualmie Falls has also been powerful in another way since 1899, when Puget Sound Power & Light (the predecessor of present-day utility Puget Sound Energy) completed construction on the region's first large hydroelectric facility there. The original powerhouse, still in operation today with much of the same equipment first installed more than a century ago, was built by boring down some 260 feet through solid bedrock before the lip of the falls to divert water over large turbines in the world's first completely underground power plant. After the diverted water goes through the underground turbines, it is released back into the river just below the base of the falls.

Eleven years later the company completed construction of a second powerhouse (this time above ground) a quarter mile downstream from the base of the falls. The whole system succeeds in keeping the hydroelectric gear generally out of sight so it doesn't detract from the natural viewscape that has been delighting people for thousands of years.

In 2004 the Federal Energy Regulatory Commission (FERC) renewed the facility's operating license for another 40 years, despite objections from the Snoqualmie Tribe regarding the diversion of water from the falls that serve as the spiritual center of their people. In 2009, Puget Sound Energy embarked on an ambitious plan to upgrade the hydroelectric and

Late afternoon golden light illuminates Salish Lodge and the hydroelectric works atop Snoqualmie Falls.

visitor facilities. Besides substantial improvements to the power-generating infrastructure there, the project—completed in 2013—also entailed major enhancements to the public recreational facilities around the falls. One of the two upper overlooks is new, along with the "River View" overlook down near the base of the falls, not to mention the paths and boardwalks linking everything up. These days the upgraded facilities pump out 54 megawatts of power while accommodating some 1.5 million sightseers every year. It certainly is a powerful place!

Beware of rainbows if visiting Snoqualmie Falls on a sunny day.

But if you would like to get more exercise, follow the path from the second upper overlook as it loops back east through Snoqualmie Falls Park's Centennial Garden—the site of many wedding ceremonies during the summer months—to a marked trailhead pointing the way down to the Snoqualmie River and an entirely different view of the falls from the bottom. Follow this steep, wide dirt trail for a half mile down into the gorge below. Enjoy the temperate rain-forest scenery—including healthy populations of iconic Pacific Northwest plants like salal, sword fern, big-leaf maples, and old-growth Douglas firs—on the way down.

Pass under some power lines transporting electricity from the Snoqualmie Falls hydroelectric project (see sidebar). Keep descending to where the trail bottoms out at the junction with a spur path leading right (north) to a lower parking lot, but follow the trail left (south) toward the lower overlook. In another tenth of a mile, continue onto a boardwalk bridge that cuts between Powerhouse #2 (built in 1910 and still in operation today) and its big green penstocks uphill to the left (east).

Follow the trail/boardwalk south, passing an overlook of the Snoqualmie River and then within another tenth of a mile, the terminus of the "River View" trail at a wooden platform overlook with a direct view of the base of Snoqualmie Falls. A sign on a chain-link fence with a locked gate warns hikers not to proceed beyond the overlook—although plenty of people seem to ignore this message and climb over anyway to splash around in the river and get closer to the base of the iconic waterfall. Spend 5 minutes or 5 hours enjoying the dynamic riparian environment before you,

Snoqualmie Falls

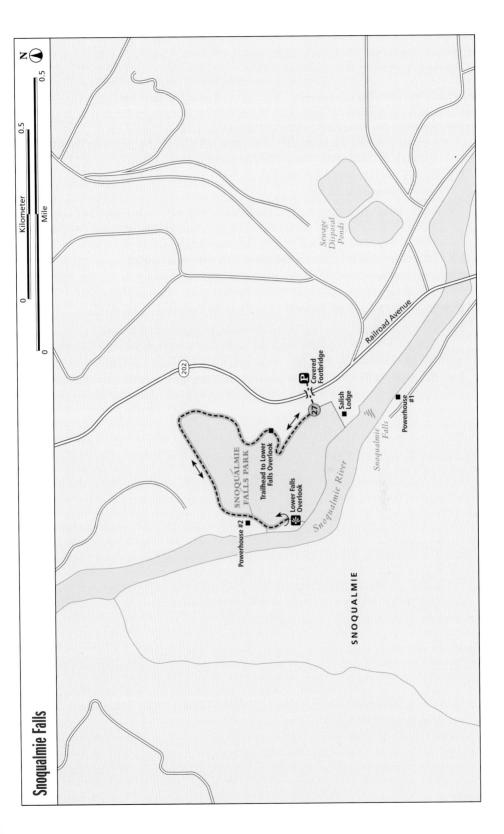

then turn around and retrace your steps back up (!) to the upper falls viewpoints and the parking lot.

Miles and Directions

0.0 Park in the free Snoqualmie Falls parking lot (GPS: N47 32.564'/W121 50.141') on the east side of WA 202 across from the Salish Lodge and cross over the road on the covered footbridge and head straight down to the overlook next to Salish Lodge.

0.1 Get your first glimpse of Snoqualmie Falls and then proceed north along the paved walk-way for more views of the falls.

0.2 Stop to admire this upper view of the falls from two overlook platforms. Retrace your steps back to the car if you've had enough, or loop through the Centennial Garden and find the trailhead leading down to the "River View" of Snoqualmie Falls.

0.5 Cross under power lines from the Snoqualmie Falls hydroelectric project.

0.65 Junction of "River View" parking lot spur trail; stay left (south) for the lower falls view, then pass between Powerhouse #2 and big green penstocks on a boardwalk/footbridge.

0.75 Check out the seemingly placid Snoqualmie River from an overlook along the trail.

1.0 Arrive at terminus of "River View" trail at an overlook of Snoqualmie Falls' base. Soak in some of the negative ions of the gorge, then turn around and retrace your steps to return back to the parking lot.

2.0 Walk back over WA 202 on covered footbridge and return to parking area, and you're done.

28 Bridal Veil Falls

Roaring out of beautiful Lake Serene above and falling more than 1,000 vertical feet across five sections, Bridal Veil Falls may be one of Washington's most dramatic cascades. It's so big that it's hard to take it all in—indeed only two of the five sections are viewable from the trail. Nevertheless, hikers interested in bathing in its glory will do just that as the falls' abundant spray is hard to avoid—and is usually a welcome relief after the switchback-laden hike up from the trailhead.

Start: Trailhead kiosk and register at south end of parking lot for Lake Serene Trail #1068. GPS: N47 48.536'/W121 34.429'

Height: 1,328 feet

Difficulty: Moderate with some steep switchbacks

Approximate hiking time: 2 hours to and from Bridal Veil Falls, out and back; 4 hours if including extension to Lake Serene

Distance: 4 miles out and back, to Bridal Veil Falls; optional extension of hike up to Lake Serene adds an additional 4 miles to the total.

Trail surface: Dirt trail and timber-hewn crib ladder steps

County: Snohomish

Land status: National forest

Trail contact: Mt. Baker-Snoqualmie National Forest, Skykomish Ranger District; www.fs .usda.gov/detail/mbs/about-forest/offices/ ?cid=fsbdev7_001655; (360) 677-2414

Maps: DeLorme *Washington Atlas & Gazetteer*. Page 47 8C

Finding the trailhead: Proceed south on Mt. Index Road from its junction with US 2 (7 miles east of Gold Bar, WA, and just before a bridge crossing the South Fork Skykomish River; if you are heading east on US 2 and get to the turn-off for the town of Index, WA, you've gone 0.3 mile too far). After 0.4 miles on Mt. Index Road, take the right fork following the sign for "Lake Serene Trail 1068" and proceed another 500 feet to the large parking area that can accommodate about 50 cars and offers up two bathroom privies. (Northwest Forest Pass at $5/day required for parking.) Look for the trailhead kiosk and register at the south end of the parking area (GPS: N47 48.536'/W121 34.429').

The Hike

Starting out at the marked trailhead with hiker's register at the south end of the Lake Serene Trail parking lot, hike up a gravel logging road on a slight grade. In 0.1 mile take the right fork in the trail. Red alders, western red cedars, big-leaf maples, devil's club, and salmonberry dominate the forest trailside as it encroaches on the roadbed. Nurse logs and standing dead tree snags provide supportive growth media for mosses, lichens, fungi, and even newer trees, not to mention great habitat for chipmunks, birds, and other forest wildlife on these flanks of Mt. Index. Follow the road as it turns into a trail, gaining 600 feet in elevation over a slow and steady climb. At a marked

Bridal Veil Creek fans out into a thundering cascade below Lake Serene on the flanks of Mt. Index.

junction 1.5 miles into the hike, head right (south) for Bridal Veil Falls (save the left fork toward Lake Serene for later).

On the way to view the falls, the trail switches back a couple of times steeply and continues up with occasional crib ladders and boardwalks to help hikers along past tougher stretches. Within another half mile of the junction, the trail delivers hikers to a fork. Go left (east), following a boardwalk toward a viewing spot of the middle section of Bridal Veil Falls. From there, head upstream (south) to view the upper section of the raging cascade, where you're sure to be covered in spray any time of year. This makes for a good lunch or snack stop, but be careful around the falls, as a bad step could be fatal. After enjoying the spray and scree atmosphere of the falls, loop back down to the junction with the middle falls boardwalk and then descend the way you came back to the junction with the trail up to Lake Serene.

If visiting Bridal Veil Falls is enough of an experience, retrace your steps back to the parking area. Those with still more energy to burn can head east for the steep hike up to Lake Serene—2 miles, 1,400 vertical feet, and more than a dozen switchbacks away. Don't be deceived by the initial quick descent down into a rock grotto where a lower-section Bridal Veil Falls rappels itself in veiling spray down a 100-foot rock face into a cliff-bottom boulder field. Enjoy a little spray and watch your step on wet rocks, then proceed east on the trail, disappearing back into deep forest cover. The lack of views only makes it easier to bear down and power through this thigh-burning section of the hike. Besides, you'll have to watch your step as roots, boulders, and fallen trees abound.

Dozens of timber-hewn crib ladders/stairs ease some of the transitions, but more than a dozen switchbacks and constant uphill hiking make the next hour of hiking feel twice as long. But within another 1.5 miles, things start to finally level off, with views opening up through occasional rock-slide chutes across the Skykomish Valley to the imposing Cascade snowpeaks to the north. It would not be a nice place to be during a storm, as evidenced by all the old tall trees leaning precariously over the ridge, some of them snapped in two and left to dangle.

Forge on and within a few hundred more feet stop at a small kiosk and trail fork with information about conservation efforts to keep the meadows surrounding Lake Serene pristine. The trail sign points left (south) down an 80-foot trail dead-ending at a backwoods "throne"-style pit toilet or straight (west) toward Lake Serene. Unless you need to go, continue straight and within another 0.1 mile you will be standing on the eerily calm shores of Lake Serene. From there, feel free to wander on the trail to its terminus at Lunch Rock on the north side of the lake by crossing a minimalist but beautiful log footbridge over the outlet for log-choked Bridal Veil Creek and

Lake Serene sits in a glacial cirque below the pointy summit of Mt. Index and above Bridal Veil Falls.

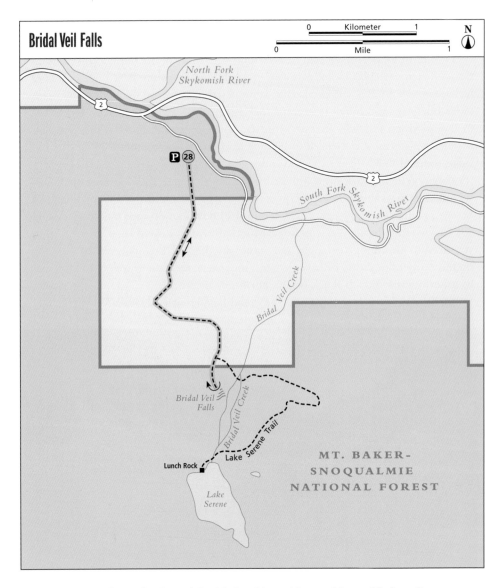

continue straight to the huge lakeside boulder with roughly an 80-foot diameter as it slopes down into Lake Serene. If it's hot and you're bold, there's no better way to cool off right quick than by jumping in the lake off of Lunch Rock. After lingering as long as necessary and perhaps enjoying a little lunch, head back toward the footbridge, following an optional 0.1-mile side spur north to an overlook of the gorge Bridal Veil Creek has created in its eons of streaming down. Otherwise, retrace your steps back down—the switchbacks seem much easier on the way down—and make your way back to the parking lot.

Miles and Directions

0.0 From the trailhead kiosk and hiker's register (GPS: N47 48.536'/W121 34.429') on the south side of the Lake Serene Trail parking lot, head south on what starts out as an old logging road but soon deteriorates into a hiking trail.

1.4 Follow the hiker's arrow sign and stay left at this junction; the logging road you have been on turns into a more traditional hiking trail.

1.5 At this signed junction go right (south) toward Bridal Veil Falls.

2.0 Arrive at Bridal Veil Falls. Spend some time exploring the middle and upper falls, then return to signed junction with trail to Lake Serene. Either return to trailhead and parking area for a total out and back hike of 4 miles, or continue up to Lake Serene . . .

2.75 Continuing up to Lake Serene, the trail passes through a rock grotto at the base of a lower section of Bridal Veil Falls, where water veils across an 80-foot cliff face.

4.5 Arrive at shoreline of Lake Serene. Enjoy the serene setting and then retrace your steps back down; no need to take Bridal Veil Falls side trail if already visited on way up.

8.0 Return to trailhead and parking lot.

29 Wallace Falls

Wallace Falls may be one of the most popular waterfalls and hikes in the state, and for good reason. The 5.5-mile out and back jaunt gets the heart racing any time of year and puts hikers in the middle of some stunning second-growth forest. The payoff, of course, is a doozy of a waterfall starting out up high as a horsetail and spreading out over the course of its first and major drop (265 feet) into a showering cascade falling into a serene-looking pool. But that's not all: The pool empties into a windy slot canyon of its own making and then spreads out and falls again before resuming a gentler course downriver.

Start: Marked trailhead at east side of Wallace Falls parking lot. GPS: N47 52.013'/W121 40.677'
Height: 367 feet
Difficulty: Moderate
Approximate hiking time: 2-3 hours
Distance: 5.5 miles out and back (including optional loop spur)

Trail surface: Dirt, rocks, and roots; hiking boots or sturdy sneakers recommended.
County: Snohomish
Land status: State park
Trail contact: Washington State Parks; www .parks.wa.gov; (360) 902-8844
Maps: DeLorme *Washington Atlas & Gazetteer.* Page 47 B7

Finding the trailhead: From Monroe, WA, head east on US 2 to the town of Gold Bar, then turn left onto 1st Street and then take the second right onto 1st Avenue West/MacKenzie Road/May Creek Road, which turns into Ley Road in three-quarters of a mile. Another half mile along, turn left onto Wallace Lake Road, then a quick right into the marked driveway entrance to Wallace Falls State Park. Stay left at the fork to continue to parking lot at trailhead (GPS: N47 52.013'/W121 40.677'). Washington State Discover Pass required for parking there (available on-site for single-day use at $10 or for an annual fee of $30).

The Hike

Hiking to Wallace Falls isn't for the faint of heart, but that said, anybody in decent shape should be able to make it just fine. A kiosk at the trailhead at the east side of the parking lot provides an overview map of the hiking route to viewpoints of both the lower and upper falls, along with an alternative route (although longer and less scenic) for those insistent on not retracing their steps. At the outset the trail is wide and flat and follows the course of some imposing towers supporting electrical lines that are carrying electricity from Columbia River dams to Western Washington. A crackling sound reminiscent of rain's pitter-patter or far-off insects is actually electricity surging through the overhead lines.

After a third of a mile under the lines, a viewpoint offers up a panorama including jagged Mt. Baring, Philadelphia Mountain, Mt. Index, and Mt. Persis. Then the trail jogs left (north), narrows, and enters into a dark second-growth forest. A hundred

Wallace Falls

Wallace Falls

feet into the woods, a sign on the right side of the trail reads, "Come forth into the light of things, Let Nature be your teacher. —W. Wordsworth." Soon thereafter, go right (north) onto the well-marked Woody Trail (at its junction with the Old Railroad Grade Trail) and cross through a 6-foot-tall wooden gate meant to deter bikes and horses. Listen for the sounds of the rushing Wallace River as they start to replace the buzzing of the power lines.

A side trail to "Small Falls" detours for 100 feet to the base of a scenic small woodland waterfall—it is usually dry by late summer. Continuing on, the Woody Trail sidles right up to the Wallace River and offers hikers the chance to dip their toes (or more) into the cold rushing water as it flows through boulder-strewn flats. From there, the Woody Trail turns left (west), leaving the river and embarking on a couple of brutal switchbacks up the side of its gorge.

At the junction with the Railroad Grade Trail, stay right (east) on the Woody Trail, which thankfully starts to descend ever so slightly, leading eventually to an overlook high above the confluence of the Wallace River and its North Fork tributary. As the Woody Trail continues northeast, it delivers hikers to a 65-foot wooden footbridge over the North Fork. Once across the bridge, look for a little side trail leading down to a riverside grotto—another good spot to cool off those aching feet or splash away the sweat.

Back on the trail, another quarter mile of hiking yields views of the lower section of Wallace Falls, sporting a 25-foot drop, from an overlook with a picnic shelter. While this makes for a good lunch or snack spot, the show isn't over. Another quarter

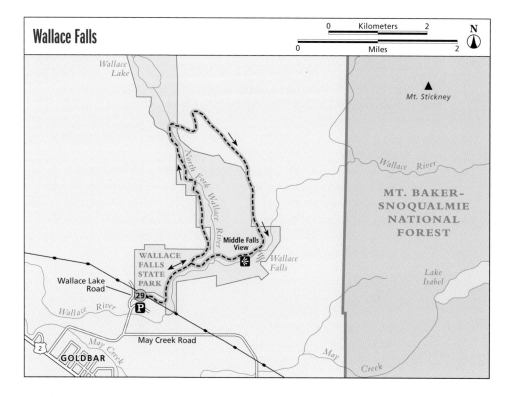

Wallace Falls

mile push gets to a viewpoint of Middle Wallace Falls, a stunning 81-foot waterfall that serves as a fine destination for those who have gone far enough. But the real treat beckons another half mile ahead. You'll have to work for it, though, as you can only see sinewy 265-foot Upper Wallace Falls if you're willing to ascend some 500 vertical feet over more than nine switchbacks on the way up to the viewpoint.

Miles and Directions

0.0 Start out at the marked trailhead (GPS: N47 52.013'/W121 40.677') on the south side of the Wallace Falls parking lot.

0.3 Check out the Cascades panorama view to the east, then follow trail north into the woods and past the William Wordsworth quotation on a sign.

0.4 Go right (north) onto Woody Trail at its junction with the Old Railroad Grade Trail and cross through turnstile gate designed to keep bikes and horses out.

0.5 Take the short marked spur trail to the left (west) to view a small waterfall (usually dry by late summer) on a creek that feeds into the nearby Wallace River. Return back to the Woody Trail and continue north. In another 200 feet look for a small rough-hewn timber stairway down to the bank of the Wallace River in case anyone needs a quick dip.

1.0 At the junction with the Railroad Grade Cut-off Trail, stay right (east) on the Woody Trail.

1.4 Stay straight/right (northeast) on the Woody Trail at a junction where the Greg Ball Trail forks off left (northwest).

1.8 Arrive at overlook of the view of Wallace Falls' lower section. Check out the covered picnic shelter, a good place for lunch, then continue over the elaborate wooden footbridge to the other side of the Wallace River.

2.1 Spy 81-foot Middle Wallace Falls from a trailside overlook.

2.75 After several switchbacks and an elevation gain of almost 500 feet from the middle falls, arrive at the viewpoint of 265-foot Upper Wallace Falls. Retrace your steps back to the junction with the Greg Ball Trail.

4.1 Take the Greg Ball Trail to the right (north) to loop back to the parking area for the sake of diversifying the scenery.

4.25 Cross through another wooden gate to leave the "hikers only" trail system and turn left (south) onto the Old Railroad Grade Trail (beware: mountain bikes and horses are allowed on this former railway thoroughfare).

4.5 Take a left (south) at the marked Railroad Grade Cut-off Trail, which cuts down steeply over 500 feet to meet the Woody Trail, where you turn right (west) and head home.

5.5 Return to trailhead and parking area.

30 Granite Falls

The South Fork Stillaguamish River drops 25 feet and then another 15 feet in its journey through the boulder-laden chute comprising Granite Falls. A fish ladder underneath the grated viewing platform along the south side of the river helps salmon make it past the modest but nevertheless daunting cascades to spawn upstream. Below the falls, calmer water makes for a nice swimming hole or a great place to launch an inner tube for a long cool slow ride farther downstream.

Start: Signed parking area ("Washington State Department of Fisheries—Granite Falls Fishway, 1954") off WA 530 (Mountain Loop Highway) 1.5 miles north of WA 92 junction at the town of Granite Falls, WA. GPS: N48 06.138'/W121 57.258'
Height: 40 feet across two drops
Difficulty: Easy
Approximate hiking time: 10 minutes

Distance: 0.2 miles out and back
Trail surface: Gravel, dirt, concrete
County: Snohomish
Land status: Washington Department of Fish & Wildlife fishway
Trail contact: Washington Department of Fish & Wildlife; wdfw.wa.gov; (360) 902-2200
Maps: DeLorme *Washington Atlas & Gazetteer*. Page 32 E4

Finding the trailhead: From Alder Street in the town of Granite Falls, drive north on WA 530 (the Mountain Loop Highway) for 1.5 miles to a parking area (about eight cars can fit) on the north side of the road under a big wooden sign marking the spot with the words "Washington State Department of Fisheries—Granite Falls Fishway, 1954." Park (GPS: N48 06.138'/W121 57.258') and walk down to the right (east) on the falls access road past the locked metal gate.

The Hike

Park in the lot on the north side of WA 530 and walk down the gated falls access road to the right (east) and then loop left (west) and follow alongside a chain-link fence separating you from Granite Falls' gorge below. While you can start to hear the falls, they are still out of sight as a result of dense greenery—including lots of invasive Himalayan blackberry plants as well as some old-growth western red cedar trees—blocking the view down into the gorge below. Continue down for about a tenth of a mile and turn right down about 70 concrete steps to a viewing platform on grates over the fish ladder, constructed in 1954 to help so-called "anadromous" fish (salmon and trout) make it upstream past Granite Falls so they can spawn and pass on their DNA to the next generation.

Walk across the grates to a railing and peer over for your first view of Granite Falls. Walk east along the grates and pavers to see the larger upper section of the falls as it tumbles 25 feet down into a bed of larger granite slabs before proceeding a few hundred feet downriver for the rest of its run. Then walk back toward the west to get

The South Fork of the Stillaguamish River zigs and zags its way through a granite gorge at Granite Falls.

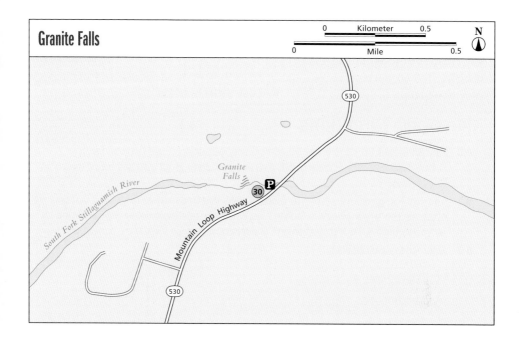

Granite Falls

0 ·······Kilometer······· 0.5
0 ·······Mile······· 0.5

N

530

Granite
Falls

30 **P**

South Fork Stillaguamish River

Mountain Loop Highway

530

HIMALAYAN BLACKBERRY: THE INVASIVE PLANT WE HATE TO LOVE

While late-summer visitors to Granite Falls will likely appreciate eating ripe blackberries from bushes growing right alongside the trail, land managers and environmentalists around the state worry that such invasive nonnative species are wreaking havoc on Washington's wildlands, wildlife, and ecosystems. Himalayan blackberry plants are some of the worst (and best-known) offenders when it comes to invasive species in Washington State. What could be so bad about a nice little plant that produces delicious edible berries in abundance? First introduced to the region more than a century ago for fruit production, Himalayan blackberry seeds and plants spread far and wide, out-competing native understory plants and preventing the establishment of native trees that need sun for germination, all the while blocking access to waterways and food sources for wildlife that can't penetrate the plants' bushy, prickly thickets. While Himalayan blackberry continues to be a big problem across the region, other problem invasive plant species include English ivy, scotch broom, Japanese knotweed, knapweed, leafy spurge, garlic mustard, and tansy ragwort, to name a few. For a more extensive list of what to look out for, or to report a sighting of any of these or other invasive species takeovers—especially around waterfalls or otherwise natural areas—contact the Washington Invasive Species Council, (360) 902-3000, www.invasivespecies.wa.gov.

a better view of the bottom section of the falls and the flatter water below—inner-tubers and splashers might be congregating there if it's a hot summer day. Be sure to stay behind the metal railing where there is one so as not to take a tumble off into the gorge. When you're done, look for the stairs back up to the access road and make your way back to the parking area via the same route.

Miles and Directions

0.0 Park (GPS: N48 06.138' / W121 57.258') facing "Washington State Department of Fisheries—Granite Falls Fishway, 1954" sign and walk down gated road to the east toward Granite Falls.

0.1 Turn right and go down a set of ~70 concrete stairs that lead down to the viewing platform above the fish ladder alongside Granite Falls. When you have explored the area alongside and below the falls enough, turn around and retrace your steps back to the parking area.

0.2 Return to the parking area.

31 Feature Show Falls

The 259-foot Feature Show Falls splits into two streams midway through its perilous descent down the gorge wall of Boulder River Canyon, showering Boulder Creek below with a constant and always refreshing spray. If it's a warm summer day, you won't be alone, as the falls is a popular place to cool off. Boulder Falls, a much smaller and less dramatic cascade, is viewable from the main trail a quarter mile beyond the turn-off for Feature Show Falls.

Start: Trailhead for Boulder River Trail 4.5 miles down French Creek Road from its junction with WA 530. GPS: N48 15.051'/W121 49.121'
Height: 259 feet
Difficulty: Easy/Moderate
Approximate hiking time: 1–2 hours
Distance: 3 miles out and back
Trail surface: Dirt trail with lots of tree roots

County: Snohomish
Land status: National forest
Trail contact: Mt. Baker-Snoqualmie National Forest, Darrington Ranger District; www.fs.usda .gov/mbs; (360) 436-1155
Maps: DeLorme *Washington Atlas & Gazetteer.* Page 32 5C

Finding the trailhead: Drive east from Arlington on WA 530 (the Mountain Loop Highway) for 19 miles and then turn right/south onto French Creek Road (also known as FR 2010) and follow it for 4.5 miles until it ends at a large parking area and the trailhead (GPS: N48 15.051'/W121 49.121') for Boulder River Trail #734.

The Hike

At the trailhead there is a small sign that says "Trail" and then 50 feet farther a kiosk with a "Boulder River Trail #734" sign, a small topo map showing where the trail goes, and a register for hikers/campers. (Note: there are no bathrooms or privies at the parking area or along the hike.) The 5-foot-wide dirt trail is wide and obviously well-used but well-maintained, with no litter in sight despite its popularity. The abundant second-growth forest tree canopy keeps the trail well shaded in the sun and relatively dry in the rain.

The trail continues along over a couple of small wooden footbridges over seasonal creeks that feed the rushing Boulder River down and to the right. Take a peek down at the river gorge by an old-growth cedar stump that serves as a nurse log for another smaller live tree, and then the trail turns left (south) and begins an uphill push. After another tenth of a mile up, the main trail turns left (south) and a side trail goes off to the right for 200 feet up to the top of a small forested butte with peekaboo views past old-growth trees over the Boulder River's gorge.

Back on the main trail, pass a sign that marks where the trail crosses into the "Boulder River Wilderness," the wilderness area within the Mt. Baker-Snoqualmie

Feature Show Falls

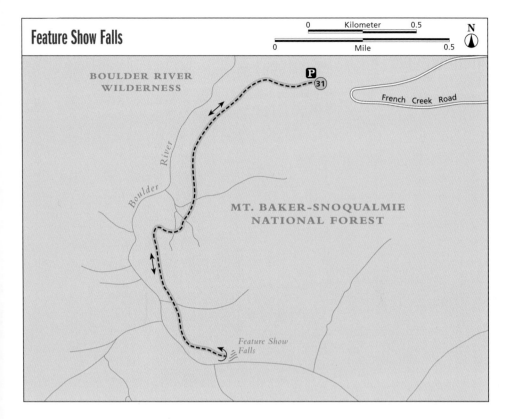

National Forest that is home to Feature Show Falls. Continuing on, the Boulder River comes into view down and to the right, accompanied by the first sounds of rushing water. Moss-festooned big-leaf maple trees dapple the trail in green light. After another quarter mile of hiking, take an obvious side trail to the right (south) that leads down to an embankment with a picture-perfect view of Feature Show Falls and then down farther to the river at the base of the falls.

On a hot day, splashing around in the river at the base of the falls is a great way to cool off. After admiring Feature Show Falls, work your way back up the side trail and then turn right (east) to continue on main trail for another quarter mile to see Boulder Falls, a smaller and much less dramatic cascade upstream from Feature Show Falls. Retrace your steps along the main trail to return to the trailhead.

Miles and Directions

0.0 Kiosk at trailhead (GPS: N48 15.051'/W121 49.121') marked with "Boulder River Trail #734," topo map of area and trail register.

0.6 Look for an old-growth cedar stump (GPS: N48 14.761'/W121 49.514') and turnout with view of Boulder River below.

Feature Show Falls

0.7 Keep left at a fork where a side trail leads right to three backcountry campsites; in another 250 feet, look for a sign on the right-hand side of trail marking the border to the "Boulder River Wilderness."

1.0 First views of the Boulder River start to show up through the trees down and to the right of the trail.

1.25 Take side trail (GPS: N48 14.480'/W121 49.319') to the right that leads to down to the Boulder River and base of Feature Show Falls. Return to the main trail and continue heading east.

1.5 Arrive at view of Boulder Falls from main trail. Turn around and retrace your route back on the main trail.

3.0 Arrive back at trailhead.

Honorable Mentions

L. Alpental Falls, Mt. Baker-Snoqualmie National Forest, WA

This dramatic 250-foot waterfall near the west summit of Snoqualmie Pass dries up by late summer, but is known to ice climbers as a great place to work on their chops in the winter. Take exit 52 (Alpental/West Summit) from I-90 and turn north onto Alpental Road, which dead-ends in less than 2 miles. The falls are visible there from the maintenance yard near the Snow Lake trailhead parking area. GPS: N47 26.998'/W121 25.367'

If you like snowshoeing or backcountry skiing, Alpental is a great place to go during the winter.

M. Otter Falls/Big Creek Falls, Mt. Baker-Snoqualmie National Forest, WA

A 10-mile out and back hike (or mountain bike ride) along a mostly level old logging road along the leafy Taylor River in the Central Cascades of Washington leads to Otter Falls, a 1,200-foot granite waterslide, and beyond that Big Creek Falls, which tumbles 238 feet down a steep stream channel clogged with fallen logs and glacial erratic boulders. From exit 34 (Edgewick Road) off I-90, turn north onto 468th Avenue SE and proceed past the truck stop and then turn right (east) onto Dorothy Lake Road, which in turn becomes Taylor River Road and then Middle Fork

Snoqualmie Road #56. Follow this for 12+ miles to a bridge over the Taylor River and stay straight at the fork, proceeding another half mile to the end of the road and trailhead. Note: The Forest Service has been working to rebuild Middle Fork Snoqualmie Road #56 due to washouts from winter storms, and expects the road to reopen at some point in 2016. GPS: N47 33.646'/W121 31.931'

N. North Fork Falls, Mt. Baker-Snoqualmie National Forest, WA

This 58-foot waterfall off WA 530 (the Mountain Loop Highway), also known as North Fork Sauk Falls, slides over a series of domed boulders and plunges into a roiling pool before turning 90 degrees and flowing downstream to another 45-foot waterfall a quarter mile downstream. From Darrington, WA, drive south on WA 530 for 15.5 miles and turn left (east) onto FR 49 at the "North Fork Sauk Falls" sign. Proceed another mile to the trailhead, park, and make the short walk down to the falls. GPS: N48 05.849'/W121 22.156'

O. Rainbow Falls, Stehekin, North Cascades National Park, WA

If you bother getting all the way to Stehekin, a land lost in time deep within Washington's Central Cascades—accessible only by ferry boat, float plane, or an exhausting multiday hike—you will definitely want to make a little extra effort to see and get sprayed by thundering Rainbow Falls as it hurtles 312 feet down a steep cliff wall into a deep plunge pool below. From the ferry landing at Stehekin, hike northwest for 3

Rainbow Falls at Stehekin

En route to Stehekin and Rainbow Falls in a Chelan Air float plane

miles along Stehekin Valley Road and look for a short spur trail to the right (north) leading down to the base of Rainbow Falls. GPS: N48 20.617'/W120 41.919'

Clear Creek Falls

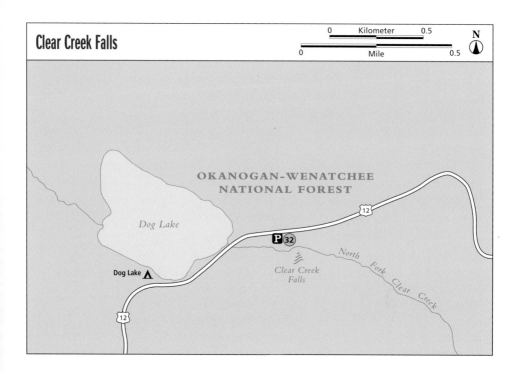

33 Snoquera Falls/Dalles Creek Falls

The 6-mile loop hike northeast of Mt. Rainier including Snoquera Falls and Dalles Creek Falls is a must-see for waterfall lovers looking to get their hearts pumping. Both waterfalls plunge over different sections of the south-facing wall of Dalles Ridge near Camp Sheppard in the Mt. Baker-Snoqualmie National Forest. Snoquera Falls, falling some 400 feet over two horsetail drops into a scree-filled rock gorge, is the main attraction of the hike, but nearby Dalles Creek Falls, tumbling 280 feet in one long, sinewy rock-hopping drop through a forested chute, doesn't disappoint either. And the huge trees, boulders, and dappled green light along the way almost make you forget what a trudge it can be to see these great waterfalls.

Start: Well-marked trailhead at east end of Camp Sheppard parking lot off WA 410. GPS: N47 02.150'/W121 33.597'
Height: Snoquera Falls: 400 feet; Dalles Creek Falls: 280 feet
Difficulty: Moderate
Approximate hiking time: 3–4 hours
Distance: 6-mile loop

Trail surface: Well-maintained dirt hiking trail through lush forest; rocks and roots are common.
County: Pierce
Land status: National forest
Trail contact: Mt. Baker-Snoqualmie National Forest, White River Ranger District; www.fs.usda .gov/main/mbs/home; (360) 825-6585
Maps: DeLorme *Washington Atlas & Gazetteer*: Page 61 E8

Finding the trailhead: The Snoquera Falls trailhead is located by the parking area (GPS: N47 02.150'/W121 33.597') at Camp Sheppard along WA 410, either 11 miles south of the town of Greenwater or 5 miles north of Mt. Rainier National Park's Stevens Canyon entrance. Northwest Forest Pass ($30/year or $5/day) required to park at Camp Sheppard lot.

The Hike

The hike to Snoquera Falls begins at the well-marked trailhead, where a sign under a kiosk points the way toward the Moss Loop Lake Trail, White River Trail 1199, and Snoquera Falls Loop Trail 1167. After passing a restroom right at the trailhead, the trail drops down into a stunning old-growth forest where huge western red cedar and Douglas fir trees are fanned by the lower-canopy, bright green leaves of vine and big-leaf maples. At the first (unmarked) junction, some 400 feet into the hike, go left, which leads past the Camp Sheppard campfire/amphitheater and soon to another trail junction, this one marked for Snoquera Falls to the left and Moss Lake Nature Trail to the right. Take the left path, which soon leads uphill into a piney forest.

After another third of a mile of hiking, at a marked junction with Buck Creek Trail 1169 take the left fork to continue east on Snoquera Falls Trail 1167. The

Accessing Snoquera Falls isn't for the faint of heart, but you just might have the majestic cataract all to yourself when you do get there.

old-growth scenery keeps getting better and better: For every huge, old-growth tree still standing, there is another fallen lengthwise across hundreds of feet of forest and serving as a nurse log for a new generation of trees. After another third of a mile, hook left/northwest at a hairpin turn in the trail right after a couple of large moss-covered glacial erratic boulders cantilevered against each other and topped off by a fallen tree.

Continue ascending and switching back along the ridge through the forest for another mile, when you will start to see peekaboo views of Snoquera Falls up and to the right. Soon you will be below the falls and an oasis-like maple grove sustained by Snoquera Creek. Resist the temptation to pick your way up toward the waterfall base through the rocks and maple trees, as an actual side trail exists a few hundred feet farther along. Take a right at this unmarked side trail and make your way through scree up to the base of the falls, as good a spot as any for a break, a snack, and a few pictures.

When you have absorbed enough of Snoquera Falls' alpine vibe, find your way through the scree back down via the side trail and turn right to continue to heading west on Snoquera Falls Loop Trail 1167 toward Dalles Creek Falls. At first, the trail will descend into the forest for a few hundred feet and then start to climb again via a series of switchbacks. In another mile, turn right/west onto Dalles Creek Falls Trail 1198 at its junction with Snoquera Falls Loop Trail 1167.

Miles and Directions

0.0 Trailhead (GPS: N47 02.150'/W121 33.597') for Snoquera Falls Loop Trail 1167 is off parking area at Camp Sheppard.

0.1 Go left at first (unmarked) junction, past amphitheater and then left again at another (marked) junction toward Snoquera Falls. In another 200 feet, go right at the (marked) junction of White River Trail 1199 and Snoquera Falls Trail 1167.

0.4 Go left toward Snoquera Falls at (marked) junction of Snoquera Falls Trail 1167 and Buck Creek Trail 1169.

0.75 Switchback to the left around two 15-foot glacial erratic boulders cantilevered against each other with a huge fallen tree over the top. Follow the trail for almost another mile up a couple of switchbacks and eventually the sight and sounds of Snoquera Falls will appear up and to the right.

1.75 After passing through an oasis-like grove of maples around Snoquera Creek below the falls, turn right/north (GPS: N47 02.361'/W121 33.263') onto the (unmarked) side trail that quickly ascends 500 feet in elevation to the base of the falls in another 0.1 mile. After checking out the falls, retrace your steps back down the side trail and turn right to continue heading west on Snoquera Falls Trail #1167 loop, which leads farther down-canyon for a few hundred feet before starting to quickly regain elevation.

3.0 At the junction (GPS: N47 02.735'/W121 33.933') of Snoquera Falls Trail 1167 and White River Trail 1199, turn right to head northwest on 1199 toward Dalles Creek Falls.

3.4 Take a right (GPS: N47 02.965'/W121 34.033') to head north onto Dalles Creek Falls Trail 1198 at its junction with White River Trail 1199. Follow for another half mile, switching back up the side of Dalles Ridge.

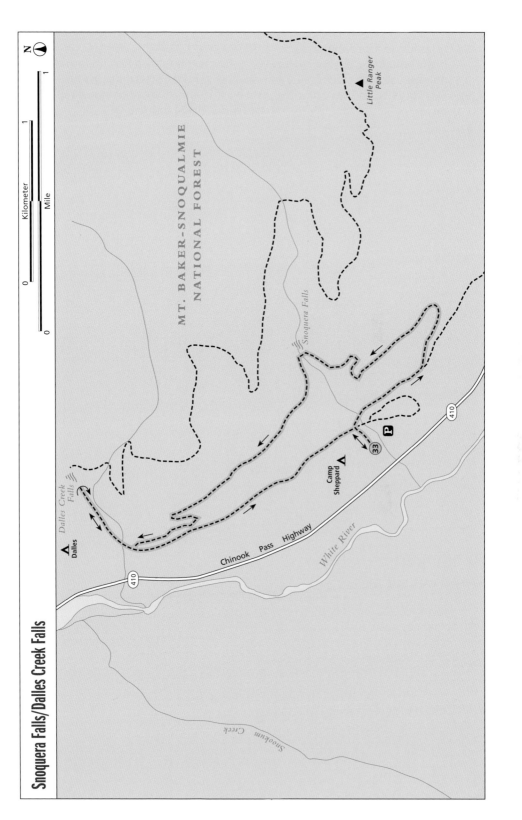

Snoquera Falls/Dalles Creek Falls

MT. BAKER-SNOQUALMIE
NATIONAL FOREST

Little Ranger
Peak

Snoquera Falls

Dalles Creek
Falls

Dalles

Camp
Sheppard

P

33

Chinook Pass Highway

White River

410

410

Snoqhum Creek

N

0 — Kilometer — 1

0 — Mile — 1

3.8 Arrive at an unmarked side trail (GPS: N47 03.087'/W121 33.814') leading to an overlook of Dalles Creek Falls from its base. After checking out Dalles Creek Falls, turn around and retrace your steps back down to the previous junction and turn left/south onto White River Trail 1199 and follow it for a mile and then turn right/south toward the trailhead at the junction with the Moss Lake Trail near the Camp Sheppard amphitheater.

6.0 Return back to the trailhead.

34 Deer Creek Falls/Stafford Falls/ Ohanapecosh Falls

This wonderful 7-mile out and back hike affords great views of three different waterfalls on three different watercourses—Deer Creek Falls on Deer Creek, Stafford Falls on Chinook Creek, and Ohanapecosh Falls on the Ohanapecosh River—as the trail zigs and zags its way south on the far east side of Mt. Rainier National Park.

Start: Owyhigh Lakes trailhead on west side of WA 123. GPS: N46 50.026'/W121 32.111'
Height: Deer Creek Falls: 62 feet; Stafford Falls: 25 feet; Ohanapecosh Falls: 50 feet
Difficulty: Easy/Moderate
Approximate hiking time: 3–4 hours
Distance: 7 miles out and back

Trail surface: Well-maintained dirt hiking trail through lush forest; rocks and roots are common
County: Pierce
Land status: National park
Trail contact: Mt. Rainier National Park, Ashford, WA; www.nps.gov/mora; (360) 569-2211
Maps: DeLorme *Washington Atlas & Gazetteer:* Page 75 8B

Finding the trailhead: Follow WA 123 for 6.5 miles south of Cayuse Pass and look on the west side of the road for a sign for the Owyhigh Lakes Trailhead (GPS: N46 50.026'/W121 32.111'); park in the pull-out across the road (there is room for about 10 cars). Pack your water bottle and lunch and cross the road to start the hike.

The Hike

From the marked trailhead along WA 123, the Owyhigh Lakes Trail descends down a well-maintained, decently graded path, with the sound of rushing water from nearby Deer Creek your constant companion. The climax forest is an amazing place, with an understory dominated by bunchberry, sword fern, and devil's club and a canopy of western hemlock, western red cedar, Douglas fir, and other iconic trees of the Pacific Northwest. After about a tenth of a mile of descending, the trail switches back to the right and soon offers up an overlook to the right of Deer Creek Falls (GPS: N46 50.056'/W121 32.224'), a thundering 62-foot cascade that has cut a zig-zag shape through a steep rock gorge. Watch your step as there is no railing and it's a long way down.

Moving on, continue for another 800 feet or so down the Owyhigh Lakes Trail until a marked junction with the Eastside Trail. Follow the Eastside Trail to the left (south) toward Ohanapecosh. Backpackers rejoice: Within 150 feet there is a marked side trail leading to Deer Creek Camp, where those properly permitted in advance by the National Park Service can spend the night. Dayhikers keep moving, and in another half mile cross a couple of streams (be prepared for the possibility of wet feet

Stafford Falls

and bring extra socks or water shoes just in case). In another two-thirds of a mile look for an unmarked but well-trodden side trail off to the left, and follow it down to view Stafford Falls, where 8-foot-wide Chinook Creek chutes 25 feet down into a woodland punchbowl roughly 50 feet across and then turns a corner and makes its way downstream less eventfully.

Continuing on, get back on the Eastside Trail and keep heading south for another mile and a third where Ohanapecosh Falls start to make itself heard and seen through the trees to the left of the trail. In another tenth of a mile, you are standing on the big wooden footbridge over 50-foot Ohanapecosh Falls. Take a few pictures and then head across the river to another vantage point 200 feet and off-trail to the left where you can view Ohanapecosh Falls in all of its two-tiered, raging glory through the omnipresent tree canopy. With three waterfalls checked off, it's time to turn around and hike back to the car.

Miles and Directions

0.0 Trailhead (GPS: N46 50.026'/W121 32.111') is well marked via a brown US Park Service "Owyhigh Lakes Trailhead" sign along WA 123, and then a mileage marker sign at the beginning of the trail proper.

0.2 View of Deer Creek Falls (GPS: N46 50.066'/W121 32.240').

0.4 Junction of Owyhigh Lakes Trail and Eastside Trail (GPS: N46 50.074'/W121 32.347'); go left (south) on the Eastside Trail.

Ohanapecosh Falls

Deer Creek Falls/Stafford Falls/Ohanapecosh Falls/Silver Falls

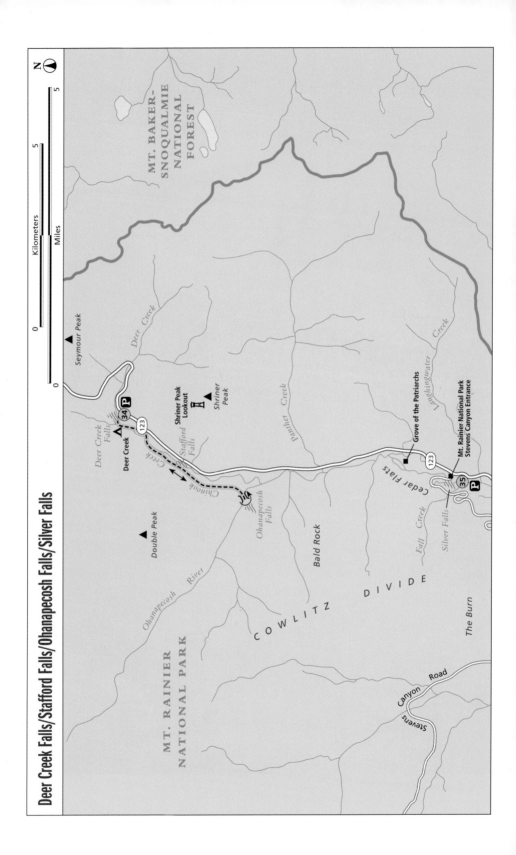

Deer Creek Falls

1.9 Follow side trail to the left (east) to Stafford Falls view (GPS: N46 49.213' / W121 33.140').

3.5 Arrive at bridge over Ohanapecosh Falls (GPS: N46 48.269' / W121 33.970'); explore views on south side of bridge, then turn around to hike back.

7.0 Return to Owyhigh Lakes Trailhead on WA 123.

35 Silver Falls

One of the more accessible waterfalls in Mt. Rainier National Park, Silver Falls chutes through a chasm of its own making in the Ohanapecosh River and then drops over a ledge, falling 40 feet into a blue-green punchbowl before continuing downstream under a wooden footbridge. Given the falls' location a short hike from the road, visitors traversing the east side of Mt. Rainier National Park shouldn't miss it.

See map on p. 168.
Start: "Silver Falls" trail sign off parking area a quarter mile south of Mt. Rainier National Park's Stevens Canyon entrance. GPS: N46 45.083'/W121 33.461'
Height: 95 feet total over four drops
Difficulty: Easy
Approximate hiking time: 15–30 minutes
Distance: 0.6 miles out and back

Trail surface: Dirt with rocks and roots, but evenly graded
County: Lewis
Land status: National park
Trail contact: Mt. Rainier National Park, Ashford, WA; www.nps.gov/mora; (360) 569-2211
Maps: DeLorme *Washington Atlas & Gazetteer*: Page 75 8C

Finding the trailhead: From Mt. Rainier National Park's Stevens Canyon entrance, drive south on WA 123 for a quarter mile and look for small parking area and "Silver Falls" trailhead (GPS: N46 45.083'/W121 33.461') on right (west) side of the road.

The Hike

To get to Silver Falls, find a small parking area a quarter mile south of Mt. Rainier National Park's Stevens Canyon entrance on WA 123 and park by a small trailhead marked with a small metal "Silver Falls" sign. Follow this boot path into the old-growth forest to the west and soon cross over the Ohanapecosh River via a high wooden footbridge and look right (north) to see Silver Falls thundering down its main 40-foot drop into a deep "blue hole" below before crashing downstream. Follow the East Side Trail north to check out the side view and top view of Silver Falls, then retrace your steps to get back to the parking area.

This hike can also be extended to include the Grove of the Patriarchs, a stunning stand of old-growth western red cedar, hemlock, and Douglas fir trees a half mile north of Silver Falls via the East Side Trail. Alternatively, hiking south from Silver Falls via the marked Silver Falls Loop Trail takes you through more verdant old-growth before delivering you to Ohanapecosh Campground in 1.2 miles. Parking at either the Grove of the Patriarchs (GPS: N46 45.469'/W121 33.446') or Ohanapecosh Campground (GPS: N46 44.245'/W121 34.030') and then accessing the Silver Falls Loop Trail on foot are also options if there is nowhere to park at the Silver Falls trailhead.

Silver Falls

Miles and Directions

0.0 Pick up the Silver Falls Loop Trail at the marked trailhead (GPS: N46 45.083' / W121 33.461') at a small parking area a quarter mile south of Mt. Rainier National Park's Stevens Canyon entrance on WA 123 and head west and then south.

0.1 Go right (north) at the fork and head north.

0.2 Follow the trail as it turns left (west) sharply and crosses the Ohanapecosh River via a wooden footbridge—look right (north) from the center of the bridge to see Silver Falls upstream—then continue upstream to view the side and then top of Silver Falls.

0.3 At the junction with the East Side Trail, turn around and retrace your steps back to the parking area.

0.6 Arrive back at the trailhead and parking area.

36 Carter Falls/Madcap Falls/Narada Falls

There's lot to do and see at Mt. Rainier National Park, but waterfall lovers will want to put the hike to Carter, Madcap and Narada Falls near the top of their bucket list. The stunning old-growth forest and serene riparian setting feels like a forgotten corner of the national park, even though the trailhead is right off the main park road and right near its biggest car campground. And if it's cloudy or raining, even better, as most of the hike is under tree cover and the lack of direct sunlight only enhances waterfall viewing.

Start: Carter Falls Trailhead on south side of WA 706, 0.1 mile south of Cougar Rock Campground turn-off. GPS: N46 45.990'/W121 47.462'
Height: Carter Falls: 53 feet; Mapcap Falls: 34 feet; Narada Falls: 176 feet
Difficulty: Easy-Moderate
Approximate hiking time: 1.5 hours one way, 3 hours for out and back round trip

Distance: 6 miles out and back (or 3 miles one way with car shuttle)
Trail surface: Well-maintained dirt with rocks and roots
County: Lewis
Land status: National park
Trail contact: Mt. Rainier National Park, Ashford, WA; www.nps.gov/mora; (360) 569-2211
Maps: DeLorme *Washington Atlas & Gazetteer*: Page 75 6C

Finding the trailhead: Drive 8 miles east of Mt. Rainier National Park's Nisqually entrance and look for the signed Carter Falls parking area on the right (south) side of the road, and look for the marked trailhead (GPS: N46 45.990'/W121 47.462').

The Hike

From the signed trailhead on the south side of WA 706 near the turn-off for Cougar Rock Campground, descend quickly into a scree field where previous eruptions of Mt. Rainier have scattered jagged rocks and boulders throughout a wide channel that serves as the riverbed for the Nisqually River on its path down from its namesake glacier above. Within a tenth of a mile, cross a 60-foot wooden-log footbridge over the Nisqually River and then find your way on the trail as it winds its way east under the evergreen forest canopy and then southeast along the Paradise River, which provides a nice aural backdrop to the hike.

Continue the gradual ascent for another mile or so through beautiful old-growth forest and eventually, after about an hour of hiking, end up at an overlook of Carter Falls, which veils out in two side-by-side segments as it bounces its way down 53 feet into a roiling pool below before rushing downstream. The only way to get a completely unobstructed look of Carter Falls would be to hike down the side of the gorge that forms it—a risky proposition at best—so unless you're an adventurer, content

The Paradise River plunges 53 feet in two side-by-side segments over lovely Carter Falls.

yourself with a view framed by trees. After drinking in the scene and perhaps eating lunch or a snack, pick up where you left off—you've got more waterfalls to see—and keep heading southeast on the trail.

Within another 0.1 mile, Madcap Falls shows itself through the trees to the right (south) of the trail as it hopscotches 34 feet down a natural rock staircase. At your own risk, climb over the rough-hewn timber fence separating you from the river to get a better look—and if you do so, be careful of slippery rocks.

Back on the trail, keep heading east and ascending with the rushing sounds of the Paradise River as your constant companion. Snow often lingers on the ground well into midsummer here. In 0.8 mile more, stay straight on the main trail at a signed junction where a spur trail splits off right (south) to some backcountry camp sites near the banks of the Paradise River. (If you are planning to camp overnight here, make sure you have obtained a backcountry camping permit in advance from any ranger station in Mt. Rainier National Park and come prepared with a tent, sleeping bag, food, and a camp stove, as no open fires are allowed at backcountry campsites.)

In another two-thirds mile, stay straight again toward Narada Falls at an intersection with the Wonderland Trail, a 93-mile boot path that encircles Mt. Rainer. A couple hundred feet farther along, the main trail hangs a right and views of Narada Falls open up to the northeast. The trail winds around to the right more and then curves up to better views of the imposing 176-foot cascade, which tumbles over a wide rock ledge and then plunges down in gushing torrents of gray-green glacial runoff. Even

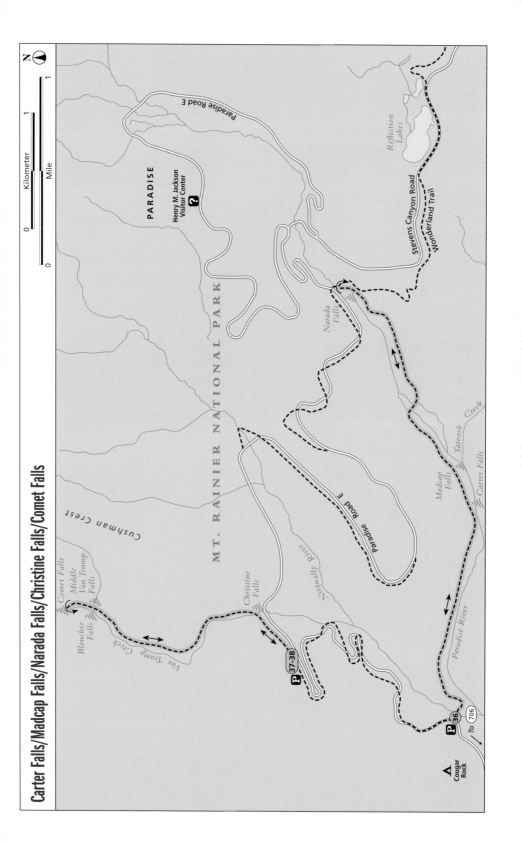

Carter Falls/Madcap Falls/Narada Falls/Christine Falls/Comet Falls

if you keep your distance of Narada Falls by staying on the trail around it, expect to get sprayed as you make your way along the rough-hewn fence protecting you from falling into the gorge below.

Make your way up and to the right along the trail and cross a wooden footbridge before reaching a stairway up to the Narada Falls parking area off WA 706 and views down on top of powerful Narada Falls. With three waterfalls and 3 miles of hiking behind you, turn around and retrace your steps back to the Carter Falls trailhead. Alternatively, if your party brought two cars along and arranged for a car shuttle, hop in and drive back down WA 706 for 6.5 miles to the Carter Falls parking lot. (Or ask one of the Narada Falls gawkers there to give you a ride down if going that way.)

Miles and Directions

0.0 Start hike at Carter Falls trailhead (GPS: N46 45.990'/W121 47.462') on south side of WA 706.

0.1 Cross log footbridge over Nisqually River.

1.25 Arrive at overlook of Carter Falls.

1.33 Arrive at overlook of Madcap Falls.

2.1 Stay straight on main trail at junction where Paradise River Camps trail spurs to the right.

2.8 Stay straight on main trail at another junction where the Wonderland Trail intersects it.

3.0 Reach the end of the trail where it intersects with WA 706 at a parking lot overlooking an automobile bridge over Narada Falls. Retrace your steps back to the Carter Falls trailhead (or spare yourself the return hike and grab a ride back along WA 706).

6.0 Return to the Carter Falls trailhead.

37 Christine Falls

Just a quick jaunt from the road and worth a stop for anyone driving by on WA 706, Christine Falls carves a sweet little niche out of the lower reaches of twisting Van Trump Creek under the graceful arch of a WPA-era stone bridge making for a perfect scene of nature framed by the works of man.

See map on p. 175.
Start: Christine Falls Viewpoint trail off parking area 2 miles east of Cougar Rock Campground on WA 706. GPS: N46 46.829' / W121 46.734'
Height: 69 feet total over two drops
Difficulty: Easy/Roadside
Approximate hiking time: 5 minutes

Distance: 0.2 mile out and back
Trail surface: Concrete pavers and dirt trail
County: Pierce
Land status: National park
Trail contact: Mt. Rainier National Park, Ashford, WA; www.nps.gov/mora; (360) 569-2211
Maps: DeLorme *Washington Atlas & Gazetteer.* Page 75 6B.

Finding the trailhead: From Cougar Rock Campground in Mt. Rainier National Park, drive east on WA 706 for about 2 miles to a bridge over Christine Falls and then turn right into the marked "Christine Falls Viewpoint" parking area (GPS: N46 46.829' / W121 46.734') on the south side of the road and access the trailhead down to the overlook below.

The Hike

Park in the Christine Falls parking area off WA 706—there is space for about a dozen cars—and look for the sign pointing the way down to the "Christine Falls Viewpoint." Follow concrete pavers down less than 200 feet to a little forest aerie tucked into the woods across from Christine Falls. Stay behind the log fence or else risk a big fall into a deep gorge. Adventurers can continue beyond the overlook on a crude and rooted path branching off down the canyon and to the south to a precipitous overlook of another smaller waterfall—approximately 30 feet high and 15 to 20 feet wide—as it shoots out of the canyon below Christine Falls.

Van Trump Creek makes its final big plunge at Christine Falls and then chutes below an impressive WPA-era stone bridge.

38 Comet Falls

Dropping 462 feet in three tiers, Comet Falls dwarfs most other waterfalls across Washington State, and getting to see it requires a short but vigorous hike along the side of the gorge formed by the twisty and often frothing Van Trump Creek. Along the way, three other waterfalls sweeten the deal and offer ample opportunities to cool off in glacier-fed waters. Those looking to get slightly off the beaten path in Mt. Rainier National Park should carve out a half-day to visit this stunning pocket of nature's finery.

See map on p. 175.
Start: Stairs up to marked trailhead at east end of Comet Falls parking lot 9.5 miles east of Mt. Rainier National Park's Nisqually entrance on WA 706. GPS: N46 46.729'/W121 47.011'
Height: Comet Falls: 462 feet; Bloucher Falls: 120 feet; Middle Van Trump Falls, 190 feet
Difficulty: Moderate
Approximate hiking time: 3 hours

Distance: 3.6 miles out and back
Trail surface: Dirt with lots of rocks and roots with footbridges, crib ladders, and stair steps
County: Pierce
Land status: National park
Trail contact: Mt. Rainier National Park, Ashford, WA; www.nps.gov/mora; (360) 569-2211
Maps: DeLorme *Washington Atlas & Gazetteer.* Page 75 6B

Finding the trailhead: Stair steps at the east end of Comet Falls parking area (GPS: N46 46.729'/W121 47.011') 9.5 miles east of Nisqually entrance to Mt. Rainier National Park.

The Hike

Find the trailhead at the east end of the Comet Falls parking area—it can fit about two dozen cars—on the north side of WA 706, about 9.5 miles east of the Mt. Rainier National Park's Nisqually entrance. Ascend some rough-hewn stair steps and then follow three switchbacks up to a ridge where the well-maintained trail assumes a slight uphill grade. At a quarter mile a big wooden footbridge crosses roiling and tumbling Van Trump Creek—look south at mid-span for a unique view of the top of Christine Falls and the iconic WA 706 automobile bridge arching above it. After crossing the footbridge, the going gets tougher with the grade increasing and the number of rocky or rooty obstacles in the trail proliferating. Glacial erratic boulders are strewn willy-nilly throughout the forest surrounding the trail.

At three-quarters of a mile, powerful-sounding Lower Van Trump Falls can be heard from the trail but is visually obscured by the sheer rock walls surrounding it. From there, the trail continues to climb with no fewer than twelve switchbacks in just a third of a mile. Mercifully all this climbing ends in a flatter, higher section of trail, yielding to a cornucopia of wildflowers and edible berries, at least in mid- to late

Bloucher Falls is a stunning, powerful cascade in its own right, but looks positively cute compared to nearby gigantic Comet Falls.

GLOBAL WARMING AND ENDANGERED WATERFALLS

Comet Falls was named after its resemblance to the tail of a streaking comet, especially in periods of peak flow. But as the Van Trump Glacier feeding the watershed below recedes in the face of global warming, the creek's flow has been reduced accordingly, and Comet Falls nowadays rarely resembles the tail of a comet.

Another notable nearby waterfall that has changed dramatically as a result of climate change is formerly robust, 680-foot Fairy Falls. Long known as the tallest waterfall in the state, these days Fairy Falls is hardly visible due to reduced flow as a result of the retreat of the Paradise Glacier that once fed it. Now Fairy Falls is reliant on snowmelt alone to keep its flow alive. And with all the hotter, drier summers we've been having lately, Fairy Falls is often all dried up by midsummer these days.

summer. (I've never seen bigger nor more abundant salmonberries anywhere anytime than on one late August hike on the Comet Falls Trail.)

After passing through this little slice of heaven, a crib ladder with nineteen huge stair steps beckons onward and upward. The Washington Trails Association helped build the crib ladder in 2012 to open up the trail after a slide made it impassable. After pausing to catch your breath after ascending the giant crib ladder, forge on for another quarter mile to a view to the west of Middle Van Trump Falls, a classic veiling cascade that anywhere else would qualify as a destination in its own right. The section closest to the trail falls 71 feet, but an upper falls visible another 50 feet up the trail tumbles 119 feet over two contiguous drops. But you haven't seen everything Van Trump Creek has to offer yet, so keep moving.

In another 0.2 mile (and 125 feet of elevation gain), arrive at the confluence of East Fork Van Trump Creek and the main channel of Van Trump Creek. The two rushing streams collide and merge in a fast and furious rock chute canyon. Then the trail crosses a wooden footbridge over East Fork Van Trump Creek with views to the northwest of Bloucher Falls, another stunning cascade falling a total of 120 feet over three stair steps.

Ascend out of Bloucher's gorge and there 500 feet down another valley is 462-foot-tall Comet Falls in all of its three-tiered glory. Hike along the east side of Van Trump Creek and note the huge old-growth fallen trees pointing downstream and others snapped off at their bases—all the result of flash debris floods during storms. In 0.2 of a mile, rejoice in the mists at the base of Comet Falls' largest upper tier on rock outcroppings above the lower tiers. Have a bite to eat and a sip of water, then turn around and head back the way you came.

Van Trump Creek starts off with a bang at Comet Falls, falling 462 feet in what original park explorers thought looked like a shooting comet's tail.

Miles and Directions

0.0 Climb up stairs at the east end of Comet Falls parking area to the marked trailhead (GPS: N46 46.729'/W121 47.011').

0.25 Cross Van Trump Creek on a big wooden footbridge, look south to see the top of Christine Falls under the WA 706 automobile bridge.

0.75 Listen for roaring Lower Van Trump Falls, which is hidden from sight by the rock walls surrounding it.

1.25 WTA-installed crib ladder with nineteen giant steps.

1.5 Middle Van Trump Falls viewpoint. Continue upstream on trail to view upper sections through the forest canopy.

1.6 Confluence of Van Trump Creek and East Fork Van Trump Creek.

1.7 Cross a wooden footbridge over East Fork Van Trump Creek and look northwest to Bloucher Falls; check out Bloucher Falls up close by exploring upstream from the footbridge, then follow the left-pointing arrow on the sign that reads: "Comet Falls: 200 feet."

1.8 Arrive at Comet Falls. Indulge in the copious spray at the bottom of the biggest drop. Return the way you came.

3.6 Get back to trailhead off WA 706.

39 Spray Falls

Spray Falls is one of the most impressive natural spectacles in Washington State as it cascades 354 feet down an andesite wall and spreads out as wide as 100 feet across by the time it reaches its base and diffuses across a wide and rocky boulder-filled gorge. The short hike to get there is well worth a couple of hours, and adventurers can tack on a visit to Spray Park a mile beyond the falls to see nearby Mt. Rainier reflected in tarns and dressed up in wildflowers.

Start: Spray Park Trailhead on the south side of Mowich Lake Campground, Mt. Rainier National Park. GPS: N46 55.959'/W121 51.800'
Height: 354 feet
Difficulty: Moderate
Approximate hiking time: 2–4 hours
Distance: 4 miles out and back for Spray Falls only; 6 miles out and back for Spray Falls and Spray Park

Trail surface: Dirt hiking path with roots and rocks; lots of switchbacks
County: Pierce
Land status: National park
Trail contact: Mt. Rainier National Park, Carbon River Ranger Station; (360) 829-9639
Maps: DeLorme *Washington Atlas & Gazetteer.* Page 74 5A

Finding the trailhead: From Buckley, drive south on WA 165 through Carbonado and then just beyond the Carbon River Gorge Bridge bear right (south) onto Mowich Lake Road, which goes another 17 miles to its terminus at Mowich Lake. Park in any of the dozens of spots available, and make sure the receipt for your Mt. Rainier National Park entrance fee ($15/car/week) is visible through your windshield. Look for the well-marked Spray Park Trail trailhead (GPS: N46 55.959'/W121 51.800') on the east side of the picnic area adjacent to Mowich Lake Campground.

The Hike

Start out at the Mowich Lake Campground, and veer right past the privies down into the forest on the well-marked Spray Park Trail (GPS: N46 55.959'/W121 51.800'). Descending down a series of a few dozen rough-hewn stair steps, the trail enters a fairyland forest of old-growth and second-growth splendor and soon crosses over Crater Creek, a rushing stream making a racket crashing over rocks and fallen logs. After a quarter mile, stay straight on the trail as it intersects with the Wonderland Trail, the 93-mile trail that circumnavigates Mt. Rainier. Hike on and in another half mile cross a small wooden footbridge over Lee Creek and look upstream at the small woodland waterfall it creates. Keep going through the thick forest, making sure to stop for an occasional delicious salmonberry or huckleberry to keep your energy level and spirits up.

In another half mile views open up to the west as the trail crosses through a rock slide area dominated by large volcanic rocks. Keep hiking as the trail tucks back into

Grant Creek starts in alpine Spray Park before dropping 354 feet right quick at Spray Falls in the less-visited northwest corner of Mt. Rainier National Park.

the forest and then go right at a marked spur trail to the right (south) and scamper down 100 feet to the Eagle Cliff viewpoint, an aerie tucked into cliffside boulders where you can spy Mt. Rainier to the east. Return to the main trail and continue hiking east. In another third of a mile stay straight on the Spray Park Trail at the junction with a spur trail that leads 500 feet down to the right (south) to several backcountry campsites and a composting "throne" in the deep, dark forest at Eagle's Roost (see sidebar; if you are planning to camp at Eagle's Roost later, you could set up your tent there now and return for the night after ascending to Spray Falls and Spray Park).

Dayhikers should push on via the Spray Park Trail for another 0.4 mile to a signed junction with the spur trail that leads down to Spray Falls. Follow the spur trail down and to the right (southeast) and across a wooden footbridge over rushing Grant Creek—check out its own mossy mini-cascade just upstream from the footbridge. Within another tenth of a mile, you'll be standing on the side of the lower section of Spray Falls, which fills up a rock slide canyon with misty spray as the water pounds down onto the rocks below. It's no wonder that an 1883 trail crew named the falls after witnessing them break "into a mass of spray."

The huge, angular volcanic rocks lining the falls' gorge make for a nice lunch spot. After relaxing by the falls and exploring around the base, retrace your steps back to the junction with the Spray Park Trail and either head southwest back to the trailhead at Mowich Lake or, if the subalpine meadows of Spray Park beckon, continue hiking

Spray Falls tumbles 354 feet down from alpine Spray Park above.

A misty rainbow shows through the spray at the base of Spray Falls.

northwest, steeling yourself for ascending some 900 feet of elevation in just a half mile of hiking via more than a dozen switchbacks.

Huffing and puffing though you might be, enjoy the changing forest landscapes as you rise up toward Spray Park. After another 0.6 mile of hiking, the topography levels out at a subalpine meadow. Cross another footbridge over a much different looking Grant Creek (you crossed it earlier via a footbridge on the Spray Falls spur trail) and make your way east into the subalpine meadows of Spray Park. If your timing is right (mid- to late summer), you will be dazzled by the wildflower show on display in every direction. If it's clear, keep Mt. Rainier's summit in view to the south; if you're lucky you may see tiny climbers' silhouettes on or near the summit.

The abundant snowmelt tarns around Spray Park make for nice rest spots, especially on a calm day when many of them reflect Mt. Rainier's glacier-clad summit in their glassy waters. The National Park Service warns that because the meadows of Spray Park are delicate and easily damaged, hikers should resist the urge to wander willy-nilly, sticking to the constructed trails and resting on rocks near the trail.

When you've soaked in as much subalpine splendor as you can handle, retrace your steps back through Spray Park and back down to the trailhead 3 miles down at Mowich Lake.

Miles and Directions

0.0 Start out on Spray Park Trail (GPS: N46 55.959′/W121 51.800′) from Mowich Lake Campground and head down into the forest via a series of rough-hewn stair steps.

0.25 Stay straight at a trail intersection with the Wonderland Trail.

0.75 Cross over Lee Creek and look upstream at the nice woodland cascade.

1.25 Cut through a boulder field from an ancient rock slide.

1.5 Go right (south) at the junction onto the spur trail to the Eagle Cliff viewpoint and walk down to the fenced cliffside overlook (GPS: N46 54.971′/W121 51.207′) with views east to Mt. Rainier. Return to the Spray Park Trail and continue east. (Ignore a marked spur trail to the south leading down 500 feet to several backcountry campsites at Eagle's Roost unless you plan to spend the night there.)

1.9 At a well-marked junction, head right (southeast) on the short spur trail down to Spray Falls.

2.0 Arrive at Spray Falls (GPS: N46 54.927′/W121 50.586′). Spend some time exploring the rocky base area and getting as close as possible to the falls before turning around and heading back to the main Spray Park Trail.

2.1 Back at the junction, go left (southwest) to retrace your steps back to the parking lot (for an out-and-back hike of 4 miles); or go right (northeast) to extend the hike to subalpine Spray Park. If you do extend the hike, steel yourself for several switchbacks to get you up to Spray Park.

Backpackers rejoice: Backcountry camping is not only allowed in Mt. Rainier National Park, but it's free—as long as you obtain a Wilderness Permit in advance or on your way to the trailhead and follow the rules (no open fires, camping only in designated backcountry campsites, and packing everything out). If you intend to spend a night or two at Eagle's Roost on the way up to Spray Falls and Spray Park, stop by the Carbon River Ranger Station (GPS: N46 59.721′/W121 54.926′) on your way in by forking left off WA 165 onto the Carbon River Road 10.25 miles south of Buckley, and follow it to its terminus at the ranger station in 7.75 miles. Permit in hand, drive back to the junction with WA 165 and turn left (east) to that road's terminus 15.5 miles later at Mowich Lake, where you can start your hike to Spray Falls.

Of course, you don't need a Wilderness Permit if you intend to camp in one of Mt. Rainier National Park's developed, car-accessible campgrounds (Cougar Rock, Ohanapecosh, and White River), where sites can be snagged on a first-come, first-served basis for $12–$15/night. Likewise, you don't need a Wilderness Permit to stay in one of the ten free walk-in tent sites at Mowich Lake Campground, a great place to spend the night if you don't feel like driving before or after an epic daylong hike up to Spray Falls and Spray Park.

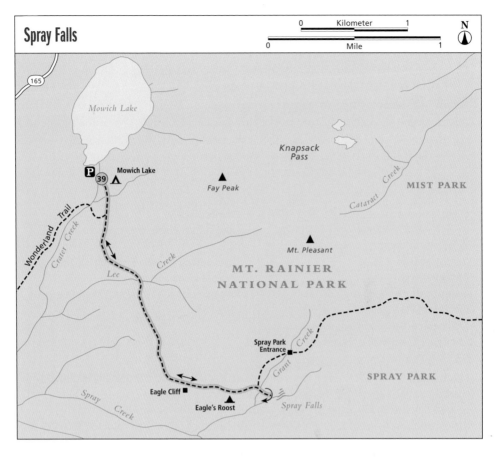

Spray Falls

2.75 Cross Grant Creek heading east on a wooden footbridge and enter Spray Park.

3.0 Find a nice tarn with Mt. Rainier's summit reflected in it and have some lunch before retracing your steps back down to the trailhead at Mowich Lake.

6.0 Return to the trailhead and parking lot at Mowich Lake Campground.

40 Tumwater Falls

Despite or maybe because of its location next to I-5 and underneath the now defunct Olympia Brewing Company, Tumwater Falls along the Deschutes River is like a breath of fresh air within its concrete jungle surroundings. It's not hard to see why this area on the outskirts of the state capitol has been a popular place for people to congregate for thousands of years; indeed the estuary by Lower Falls was the site of one of the largest Native American settlements in the region long before the pioneer days and white settlement.

Start: Tumwater Falls parking lot. GPS: N47 00.802'/W122 54.248'
Height: Upper Falls: 18 feet; Middle Falls: 10 feet; Lower Falls: 26 feet
Difficulty: Easy
Approximate hiking time: 20 minutes
Distance: 1-mile loop
Trail surface: Gravel and dirt paths, pavement, metal grates, and wooden boardwalks

County: Thurston
Land status: Private land operated as a public park
Trail contact: Olympia Tumwater Foundation; www.olytumfoundation.org; (360) 943-2550
Maps: DeLorme *Washington Atlas & Gazetteer.* Page 58 5F

Finding the trailhead: Heading south on I-5 from Seattle, take exit 103 and turn left (east), crossing over the highway and the Deschutes River canyon on Custer Way SW. Take your next right (south) onto Boston Street SW, which runs downhill and then curves right (west) and again crosses the river, this time on a smaller bridge. Take a left at the "T" to head southbound on Deschutes Way SW and then 0.2 mile later take another left (east) onto C Street SW, which leads to the well-marked entrance to the parking area for Tumwater Falls Park (GPS: N47 00.802'/W122 54.248'). If you are coming from the south on I-5, take exit 103 right onto Deschutes Way SW and then take your third right (east) onto C Street SW, and the park entrance will be down on your left (north) 300 feet (GPS: N47 00.802'/W122 54.248').

The Hike

Park in the Tumwater Falls parking lot (GPS: N47 00.802'/W122 54.248') and walk north into the adjacent park. Pass by the park headquarters building (where public bathrooms are available) and then check out a restored 80-foot-tall Native totem pole that originated on Kingcome Inlet on coastal British Columbia. Following the siren song of rushing water, continue north to the grates that cover the upper section of fish ladders installed in 1952 that have been helping salmon over the falls ever since. Keep walking down and look to your right (east) to see Upper Falls, half of which has been obviously augmented by the hand of man so fish can get around while the other half remains a natural cliff where the Deschutes River drops off 18 feet before rushing downstream.

An old wooden footbridge crosses right over Lower Tumwater Falls.

From there, the trail zigs and zags down along the west side of the Deschutes River, passing by the Washington Salish Native Plant Garden (see sidebar) on your left (west) and a bridge over the river to the right (east), which you can save for later when you loop around upon your return to the car.

At about a third of a mile into the walk, stop off at a concrete overlook with a view of the modest 10-foot Middle Falls, a rolling and tumbling section of the river

CELEBRATING NATIVE PLANTS AT TUMWATER FALLS

If you like cultural and/or natural history, spend some time checking out the Washington Salish Native Plant Garden, dedicated in 2012 near the upper section of Tumwater Falls (across the river from the brewery). A joint project of the Olympia Tumwater Foundation and three regional Salish Indian tribes (Squaxin Island, Chehalis, and Nisqually), the garden features upward of fifty-six indigenous plant species traditionally used by Native Americans across the region for food, medicine, clothing, tools, and even art. Northwest gardeners and backcountry hikers alike will be familiar with many of the beautiful and functional plants there. Keep an eye out for bees and hummingbirds, as both are attracted to the colorful concentration of native plants. Interpretive panels at the base of the garden identify the plants therein and explain how the garden came to be.

WHAT'S BREWING AT TUMWATER FALLS

The history of brewing at Tumwater Falls dates back to 1896 when German immigrant Leopold Schmidt, already operating a successful brewery in Montana, traveled on business to Olympia and identified the springs around nearby Tumwater as an exceptional water source for making beer. He sold his Montana brewery and moved lock, stock, and barrel to Tumwater, buying 5 acres along the Deschutes River around Tumwater Falls and setting up shop as the Olympia Brewing Company. When the Klondike Gold Rush hit the next summer, Olympia Brewing Company was poised to make a killing shipping beer up to thirsty gold miners in Alaska—and "Oly" beer has been a Northwest icon ever since.

Schmidt went on to run the brewery successfully until his death in 1914, just weeks before Washington went "dry" as part of the national prohibition movement. Under the leadership of Schmidt's sons, the company hung on for a while making fruit juices and jams, but eventually shuttered operations entirely. The sons sold off the old brick brewhouse on Middle Falls and moved onto other ventures.

But with the repeal of prohibition 19 year later, the family reorganized the company and started brewing beer again on Tumwater Falls out of a brand new brewery upstream from the original brewhouse. Members of the Schmidt family owned and operated the company until 1983, when it sold to G. Heileman Brewing Company and then to a succession of subsequent owners culminating with Miller, which shut down the Tumwater Falls brewery in 2003, citing the financial inefficiencies of operating such a small-scale facility. But Oly lovers can still grab a can of their favorite creamy golden lager—*Men's Journal* named it one of the world's twenty-five best beers in a 2012 round-up—at select bars and beer stores, even if it is brewed nowadays in Wisconsin.

where Olympia Brewing Company's original brewhouse stood before the company moved its operations upriver above Upper Falls (see sidebar). Continuing north on the trail on the west side of the river, leave a footbridge that crosses the river to your right—you'll come back later to cross it when you loop back on the other side of the river. But for now, zig-zag down a series of stairs and then turn right at the bottom for a picture-postcard view of Lower Falls (GPS: N47 01.101'/W122 54.240') and the quaint wooden footbridge above it. Expect to get wet from Lower Falls' abundant spray. Snap a few pics and then head over to the nearby 70-by-30-foot concrete patio looking north out onto Capitol Lake, a placid estuarine scene below Lower Falls, which a few hundred years ago was the site of one of the biggest Native settlements in the region.

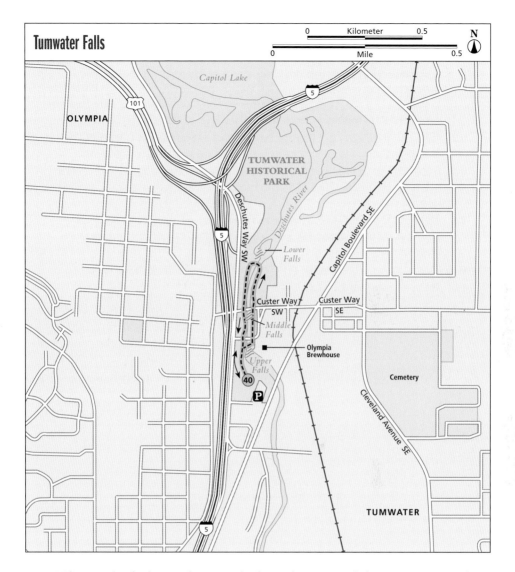

When you've had enough, return back up the steps and then cross over to the east side of the river via the 120-foot wooden footbridge that crosses over the top of Lower Falls—be sure to look down from the middle for a unique view on the pretty little waterfall. After crossing over, turn right (south) and head down the east side of the river to get new perspectives on Middle Falls and Upper Falls. Cross back over to the west side of the river on the footbridge by Upper Falls that you skipped on the way to Lower Falls, then return back to the parking lot.

Miles and Directions

0.0 Starting out from the Tumwater Falls Park parking lot (GPS: N47 00.802' / W122 54.248'), walk north across park grounds and check out the park headquarters building and a Native totem pole before making your way toward views of the fish ladder and Upper Falls. To make it a loop hike, resist the urge to cross the upper footbridge (you'll come back over it later) and head north along the west side of the river.

0.25 Walk under the Custer Way SW bridge that you drove over on your way to the park. Continue on and check out a concrete overlook down at the water level of Middle Falls.

0.4 Follow concrete stairs on west side of river as they zig-zag down to the overlook of Lower Falls (GPS: N47 01.101' / W122 54.240') and the southern section of Olympia's Capitol Lake.

0.5 After crossing over the lower footbridge and hiking south on the east side trail, follow a short spur trail to the riverside for a close-up view of the Deschutes before it goes over Lower Falls.

0.75 Cross back over to the west side of the river on the upper footbridge below Upper Falls.

1.0 Return to the parking lot.

Honorable Mentions

P. Falls Creek Falls, Mt. Rainier National Park, WA

This 45-foot waterfall chutes out of the side of a cliff, falling in two tiers and practically spraying WA 706 as cars rush by below. Worth a quick stop-and-look if you're driving by. From Mt. Rainier National Park's Stevens Canyon entrance, drive east on WA 706 for 0.25 mile to the Falls Creek Bridge and Falls, marked by a small roadside sign. Pull off on either side of the bridge and climb down to the bottom of the falls, then climb midway up for additional views. GPS: N46 45.917' / W121 33.635'

Falls Creek Falls couldn't be more convenient as it horsetails and then veils down 45 feet right off WA 706 near Mt. Rainier National Park's Stevens Canyon entrance.

Q. Skookum Falls, Mt. Baker-Snoqualmie National Forest, WA

This 250-foot, two-tiered waterfall northeast of Mt. Rainier National Park can be seen at a distance right from the side of WA 410 or can be accessed close-up via a pleasant 4-mile out-and-back hike from the trailhead on FR 73. From Greenwater, WA, drive south on WA 410 for 9.5 miles to the signed "Skookum Falls" viewpoint and look east for the falls about a quarter mile away across the White River. Or to make a hike of it and get up-close-and-personal views, drive another 1.7 miles farther south just beyond the Camp Sheppard turn-off and look for the marked trailhead on the east side of WA 410. Park and follow the trail into the forest, crossing over the White River before turning right (north) and hiking for 2 miles to the base of Skookum Falls. GPS: N47 03.023'/W121 34.593'

R. Wilson Glacier Falls, Mt. Rainier National Park, WA

This imposing 315-foot-tall, 75-foot-wide waterfall crashes over a cliff at the foot of the Wilson Glacier on the flanks of Mt. Rainier. Only ice climbers and helicopter passengers can access Wilson Glacier Falls close-up; the rest of us will have to be content hiking in 1.25 miles on the Skyline Loop Trail from Paradise for far-off views of the massive glacial torrent. From Elbe, WA, drive east on WA 706 for 13.8 miles and enter Mt. Rainer National Park's Nisqually entrance (entrance fee of $15/car/week, or $30/year), and continue east for another 17.7 miles to the Paradise parking lot. The trailhead for the Skyline Loop Trail is on the north side of the upper parking lot at Paradise next to the Henry M. Jackson Memorial Visitor Center there. GPS: N46 48.753'/W121 44.789'

S. Rainbow Falls State Park, Dryad, WA

While Rainbow Falls may only drop about 5 feet, the surrounding 139-acre park grants visitors access to miles of hiking trails through some of the only old-growth forest left standing around Olympia, not to mention the opportunity to swim (and fish) in the flats of the Chehalis River. To get there, take exit 77 off I-5 and head west on WA 6 for 16 miles to the Rainbow Falls State Park entrance (Discover Pass required, $10/day or $30/year). Rainbow Falls and surrounding swimming and fishing holes are adjacent to the bridge crossing the Chehalis River en route to the campground. GPS: N46 37.785'/W123 13.971'

Southwest Washington

Southwest Washington may actually be the least-known part of the state, but those who love wilderness, mountain vistas, and natural history will feel right at home. While this part of the state may share a similar topographic profile and geologic past with neighboring regions of Washington and Oregon, the presence of still-active Mt. St. Helens there makes for interesting times—especially because the volcano reawakened a few years back and is currently in an ongoing

Mt. St. Helens casts a long shadow over Southwest Washington.

Standing dead tree in the Mount Margaret Backcountry with a backdrop of Spirit Lake and Mt. St Helens

dome-building phase. Touring through the blast zone from the big 1980 eruption there is an amazing experience, as much for the still-visible destruction as for the natural regeneration that has taken place in the intervening three decades. And while waterfall lovers may be familiar with the Oregon side of the Columbia River Gorge, let's not forget that Southwest Washington borders the same river and has several of its own waterfalls there on offer.

Camping and Accommodations

Carson Ridge Luxury Cabins: The perfect home base for time spent hiking around the Columbia River Gorge. Each private cabin is one of a kind, featuring handmade beds, gas fireplaces, and satellite televisions, among numerous other amenities. A soul-satisfying gourmet breakfast is served up every morning in the main dining room or hand delivered to your cabin. 1261 Wind River Hwy., Carson, WA 98610. (877) 816-7908, www.carsonridgecabins.com

Skamania Lodge: Skamania Lodge was built in 1993 to resemble the great lodges of the early 1900s. In true Northwest fashion, resource reclamation was at the heart of construction. The Cascade-style Skamania Lodge features giant timber columns taken from the old Bumble Bee cannery in Astoria. The 254-room lodge offers fine and casual dining, golf, a spa and fitness center, and even an on-site US Forest Service

Information Center. 1131 SW Skamania Lodge Way. Stevenson, WA 98648. (509) 427-7700, www.skamania.com

Lower Falls Campground: Steps away from Lower Lewis River Falls and the trailhead for the Lewis River hike. The campground has forty-three first-come, first-served sites, restrooms, water, and is open from May until October. $15/night. (360) 891-5000, www.fs.usda.gov/recarea/giffordpinchot/recreation/camping-cabins/recarea/?recid=31590&actid=29

Iron Creek Campground: Set in some of the best old-growth forest you could imagine, the campground is open from late May to late September. Ninety sites, water and restrooms. Fees are subject to change, typically $15 a night. (360) 891-5000, www.fs.usda.gov/recarea/giffordpinchot/recarea/?recid=31306

Beacon Rock State Park: Direct access to the Hardy Falls/Rodney Falls hike. The park has twenty-six tent sites ranging in price from $12–$42/night depending on season and amenities. Limited winter camping is available; check with the park. (509) 427-8265, www.parks.wa.gov/474/Beacon-Rock

41 Siouxon Creek Falls

The Siouxon Creek drainage (pronounced sou-sawn, rhyming with Tucson) is situated south of Mt. St. Helens in the wonderfully vast Gifford Pinchot National Forest. The forest is an attractive combination of 100-year-old post-forest-fire regrowth and ancient snags, both upright and fallen. The understory is lush and the waters of Siouxon Creek collect in deep, inviting pools of green and blue. The area is also chock-full of waterfalls. There are a number of options with regards to length of hike, which make it great for anything from a quick family-friendly jaunt up to an overnight backpacking excursion.

Start: Trailhead at dead end of FR 5701. GPS: N45 56.790' / W122 10.671'

Height: Horseshoe Creek Falls: 57 feet; Siouxon Falls: 28 feet; Chinook Falls: 62 feet; Wildcat Falls: 124 feet of visible drop

Difficulty: Easy/Difficult (depending on route choice)

Approximate hiking time: 1.5–8 hours

Distance: 9-mile semi-loop or 10.8-mile out and back to Wildcat Falls; 8.4-mile out and back to Chinook Falls; 4-mile out and back to Siouxon Falls

Trail surface: Hard-packed dirt, duffy, rocky

County: Skamania

Land status: National forest

Trail contact: Mt. St. Helens National Volcanic Monument; www.fs.usda.gov/mountsthelens; (360) 449-7800

Maps: DeLorme *Washington Atlas & Gazetteer*: Page 88 F2

Northwest Forest Pass or $5 day-use fee may be required but is not at this time.

Finding the trailhead: From Portland, take I-205 north to WA 500 East. Travel along this road that soon becomes WA 503. Make a left to stay on stay on WA 503 North, through the towns of Battle Ground and Amboy. Just past the Mt. St. Helens National Monument Headquarters, turn right onto NE Healy Road. After 9.2 miles bear left at a fork heading uphill onto FR 57. After 1.2 miles, turn left onto paved FR 5701. Drive 3.7 more miles to where the road dead-ends at the trailhead (GPS: N45 56.790' / W122 10.671'). The trail heads down into the forest about 100 feet before the end of the road. Be forewarned, there are a number of "gotcha" potholes and dips along the last 10 miles or so to the trailhead.

The Hike

First and foremost, this hike can be an easy-to-moderate outing or a potentially adventuresome, creek-fording wilderness trek. A lot is going to depend on your willingness to get wet and the time of year you visit. You will potentially make three creek crossings. Fording the creeks during spring, especially the third fording of Siouxon Creek, can be dangerous. Please exercise caution. While all three fords are relatively easy-peasy by late summer in terms of water level, rocks are still slippery. Please be aware of this beforehand if your goal is to reach Wildcat Falls.

Siouxon Creek Falls drops 28 feet into an inviting splash pool.

From the trailhead, descend a quick 50 feet before encountering the first trail junction. Stay right here and follow the somewhat steep path down to a bridged crossing of West Creek. Once across the creek you'll note the first in a series of excellent campsites that will spring up along the trail every so often. You'll also get your first taste of the predominant character of this hike: well-graded, rolling trail that gracefully gains and loses elevation. The path gives almost constant creek views from above and verdant forest below.

Keep hiking past a junction with the Horseshoe Ridge Trail and arrive at Horseshoe Falls at the 1.6-mile mark. A bridge carries you over a deep chasm just above the falls. There are some steep viewpoints accessed on either side of the falls. Continue past another set of campsites a short 0.4 mile more to Siouxon Falls. The scenic falls pour into a very inviting splash pool. Access is steep and potentially slippery here. If swimming is the main reason for creek access, there are better spots along the creek earlier and later on.

To continue the hike to Chinook Falls and potentially Wildcat Falls, keep hiking to an easy-to-miss junction with the Wildcat Trail at the 3.2-mile mark. This trail descends down to the creek and will potentially be the place you ford Siouxon Creek later on. If your goal is to do the 9-mile semi-loop, you might be interested in taking the short path down to the creek and assessing the water levels. Keep in mind that if you're attempting to make it to Wildcat Falls and do not ford here, later on you must backtrack and hike a total of 10.8 miles back to the trailhead. If your goal is only to Chinook Falls, pay this junction no mind.

For now, continue hiking along Siouxon Creek past another junction with the Horseshoe Ridge Trail and arrive at a mini-creek that crosses the trail. It is beautiful but dangerous. There is an alluring small falls just upstream, but keep your eyes on the trail when crossing. It is slick! A short distance beyond this crossing you'll reach the bridge that spans a narrow gorge and heads to Chinook Falls. It's worth noting that 14 Mile Falls can be seen just upstream from the bridge. Please also note that at the time of publication, this bridge is closed. The creek is potentially fordable upstream from 14 Mile Falls. Again, exercise caution and check with the Forest Service before you go.

After the bridge the trail continues past another set of fine campsites and quickly descends to Chinook Creek near the base of Chinook Falls. The trail peters out as it gets closer to the falls. If this is your goal, turn around and head back the way you came. If you're proceeding on to Wildcat Falls, ford the creek here and pick up the trail on the other side. A downed log makes for a potentially easier crossing in high water season. Two-tenths of a mile after the ford, stay straight at a junction and continue along the Wildcat Trail for a total of 0.8 mile from Chinook Falls to a crossing at Wildcat Creek. Make your way over a set of very large downed logs and pick up the trail on the other side of the creek.

Almost immediately you'll reach another junction. Stay right and ascend a short 0.3 mile along the strikingly beautiful creek to a viewpoint of Wildcat Falls, passing a handful of cascades along the way. There is no need to go beyond the viewpoint that occurs at a steep switchback, so head back down to the junction and make a sharp right turn down to Siouxon Creek. Again, this is the most difficult crossing when water is high, so be careful. Alternately, you can backtrack the way you came, eventually making it back to the trailhead.

If you ford the creek here, pick up the trail on the other side and a short distance later arrive at the Siouxon Creek Trail. Hang a right here and hike back to the trailhead, passing Siouxon and Horseshoe Falls in the process.

Miles and Directions

0.0 From the trailhead (GPS: N45 56.790'/W122 10.671'), descend 50 feet to a junction. Turn right onto the Siouxon Creek Trail and continue descending steeply toward the creek.

0.3 Continue straight over a footbridge across West Creek.

1.1 At a junction with Horseshoe Ridge Trail, continue straight.

1.6 Arrive at Horseshoe Falls (N45 57.340'/W122 09.244'). Enjoy the views and then continue hiking.

2.0 Arrive at Siouxon Falls (N45 57.570'/W122 09.108'). Retrace your steps back to the trailhead or continue hiking.

3.2 Arrive at easy-to-miss junction with Wildcat Trail on the left. Continue straight on the Siouxon Creek Trail, passing another junction with the Horseshoe Ridge Trail.

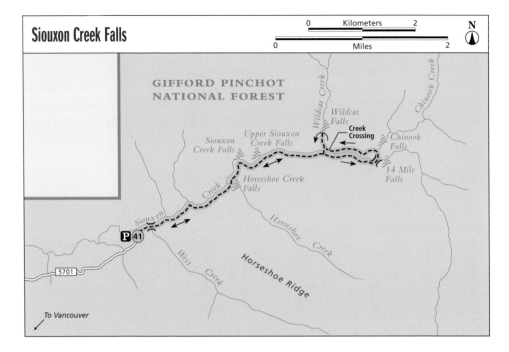

Siouxon Creek Falls

GIFFORD PINCHOT
NATIONAL FOREST

Wildcat Creek

Chinook Creek

Wildcat Falls

Creek Crossing

Upper Siouxon Creek Falls

Siouxon Creek Falls

Chinook Falls

14 Mile Falls

Horseshoe Creek Falls

Siouxon Creek

Horseshoe Creek

West Creek

Horseshoe Ridge

P 41

5701

To Vancouver

3.9 At a slippery mini-creek crossing (N45 57.583'/W122 07.024'), continue a very short distance to a bridge crossing. Note 14 Mile Falls (N45 57.599'/W122 06.965') just upstream. Cross the bridge and continue straight.

4.2 Arrive at Chinook Falls (N45 57.771'/W122 06.916'). Turn back or ford creek, pick up trail on the other side and continue hiking.

4.4 At the next trail junction, stay left and continue.

5.2 Cross Wildcat Creek by scaling large logs, fording the creek, and picking up the trail on the other side. Continue a few dozen feet to another junction and make a right, ascending to Wildcat Falls.

5.5 Arrive at Wildcat Falls Viewpoint (N45 57.905'/W122 07.829'). Head back 0.3 mile to the previous junction. Make a hard right and quickly arrive at Siouxon Creek. If water is too high, head back the way you came to the trailhead. If fordable, cross the creek here, pick up the trail, and hike a short distance to the junction with the Siouxon Creek Trail.

5.8 At a junction with the Siouxon Creek Trail, turn right and head back to the trailhead.

9.0 Return to the trailhead.

42 Angel Falls Loop

The Angel Falls Loop Hike is an amusement park ride for outdoor lovers. This diverse walk in the woods starts unassumingly enough with a long, steady ascent before skirting around massive cave-laden cliffs and descending down to lush grottoes highlighted with waterfalls. The hike then levels off through pleasant woods rich with red huckleberries before a final drop and return back to the trailhead.

Start: Burley Mountain Trailhead on FR 28. GPS: N46 25.773' / W121 50.798'
Height: Angel Falls: 150 feet; Bridal Veil Falls: 195 feet over three drops; Covell Creek Falls: 75 feet
Difficulty: Easy
Approximate hiking time: 1–2 hours
Distance: 2.6 miles
Trail surface: Hard-packed dirt, duffy, rocky

County: Lewis
Land status: National forest
Trail contact: Gifford Pinchot National Forest, Cowlitz Valley Ranger District, Randle, WA; www.fs.usda.gov/recarea/giffordpinchot/recreation/recarea/?recid=31180; (360) 497-1100
Maps: DeLorme *Washington Atlas & Gazetteer*. Page 88 B5

Finding the trailhead: From Randle, drive south on WA 131 toward Mt. St. Helens for 1 mile and turn left (east) onto FR 23 toward Trout Lake. Follow FR 23 for ~12 miles then turn right (south) onto FR 28 (Cispus Road) and follow it as it heads south then curves to the west, crossing over Yellowjacket Creek after about 1.3 miles and turning from pavement to gravel. Continue on FR 28 for another 0.9 mile and park at a small parking pull-out on the left (north) side of the road. Cross to the south side of the road and look for the easy-to-miss Burley Mountain trailhead (GPS: N46 25.773' / W121 50.798').

The Hike

Start by crossing FR 28 from the parking pull-out and picking up the marked Burley Mountain trail. The path ascends steadily, without pause for half a mile to a junction, where you'll take the path down to the right (west). Follow the trail as it makes its way around a massive rock wall, skirting cliff faces and passing by a number of what look like critter-housing caves. The trail never gets too dicey, even for those who struggle with heights or exposure. After another half mile, turn left (south) at a junction leading to Covell Creek Falls.

The often slippery, spray-glazed path leads behind and underneath Covell Creek Falls. The 75-foot cascade tumbles down in two distinct streams split by a rock at the jumping off point of the falls. Past the falls, the path again gains elevation in a hurry, following a handful of switchbacks up to the next junction.

Hang a left (east) here and descend down toward the water again, arriving at a creek crossing and the base of Angel Falls. Enjoy the blissful forest scene, then rock-hop past the base of Angel Falls and arrive in short order at another creek crossing.

Follow the trail right under where Covell Creek Falls' double horsetails join together in midair after pouring off the protruding cliff wall above.

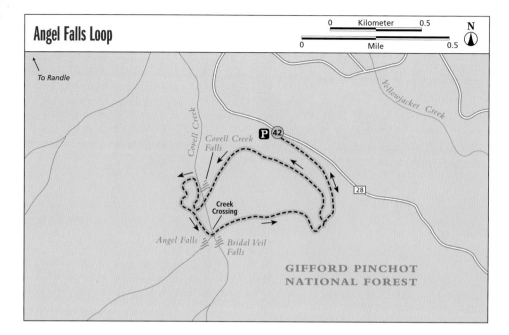

Angel Falls Loop

To Randle

Covell Creek

Covell Creek Falls

P 42

Creek Crossing

Angel Falls

Bridal Veil Falls

28

Yellowjacket Creek

GIFFORD PINCHOT
NATIONAL FOREST

If you're interested in checking another waterfall off your to-do list, follow the boot path upstream for about 300 feet to the base of Bridal Veil Falls.

Head back to the main trail and cross the creek, picking the trail up on the other side. The path now follows a mainly level, straight line through a pleasant forest that bursts at the seams with red huckleberries in mid- to late summer. The trail eventually begins a steady downhill run and arrives at the first junction of the hike. Stay straight here and continue the steady descent back down to the trailhead.

Miles and Directions

0.0 From the trailhead (GPS: N46 25.773'/W121 50.798'), hike 0.5 mile to a junction.

0.5 Go right and continue hiking along rock cliffs for another 0.5 mile and arrive at another junction.

1.0 At a junction, turn left toward Covell Creek Falls.

1.1 Arrive at Covell Creek Falls. Continue hiking.

1.5 At a junction, turn left and descend down to Angel Falls.

1.7 Arrive at Angel Falls. Continue hiking.

1.8 Get to Covell Creek and head upstream along a boot path for 300 feet to Bridal Veil Falls. Backtrack, cross the creek and continue hiking.

2.2 Arrive back at the first junction of the hike. Stay straight and continue back down to the trailhead.

2.6 Return to the trailhead.

BRYAN SWAN: THE WATERFALL CHASER

Growing up in Western Washington, Bryan Swan always loved waterfalls. Frequent childhood trips into the North Cascades and other wild areas of the region cemented his appreciation of nature and fast-moving water. During high school in the late 1990s, he decided to combine his passion for exploring waterfalls with his interest in web programming, and the Northwest Waterfall Survey, a comprehensive and free online database of waterfalls across Washington, Oregon, and Idaho, was born.

"When I started out researching waterfalls, it was mainly by scouring encyclopedias and World Books for 'tallest of' lists, and then when I started finding various guidebooks, it just stoked the fire," he says. "Greg Plumb's *Waterfall Lover's Guide to the Pacific Northwest* was my biggest inspiration as a kid, so when I was able to grab hold of a medium with which I could share my findings, there was no looking back at that point."

These days Swan's "baby" contains information and photographs on more than 3,000 Pacific Northwest waterfalls (1,800+ are in Washington State), all of which he has visited personally. "I have time for all the waterfall hunting I guess because I'm not married and don't have kids, so it's pretty easy to make time," he reports. "I'm usually out taking pictures or hunting down waterfalls every weekend unless the weather is particularly inclement—at least outside of the winter months."

Swan set up the Northwest Waterfall Survey so that he must personally visit any entry to measure it properly and give it a rating according to his scale, but he does welcome help in the form of "any first, second, or through-the-grapevine beta" that other waterfall lovers can provide from their own excursions: "Access issues, locations of waterfalls I'm not certain about or don't have listed at all, whether a particular waterfall dries out in the summer, whether it's currently flooding, and especially any historical information pertaining to the discovery and naming of any waterfall would be much appreciated."

Beyond the Northwest, Swan also helped launch the World Waterfall Database in 2006 with his friend northeastern US waterfall expert Dean Goss. Currently this combined effort provides information on more than 13,000 waterfalls around the world (although more than 80 percent of the listings are in the United States). Swan and Goss are working hard to expand the World Waterfall Database—especially international coverage—through crowd-sourced information gathering and other networking techniques only possible due to the reach and connectedness of the Internet.

43 Lewis River Falls

With six waterfalls of consequence along the route, this hike along the Lewis River is a must-do for any self-respecting waterfall lover. The three major cascades of the outing, Upper, Middle, and Lower Lewis River Falls, are all unique and truly headliners in their own right. The lower falls are one of the most accessible, photogenic, and visited falls in the Gifford Pinchot National Forest. And justifiably so.

Start: Lower Falls Recreation Area Day Use parking lot. GPS: N46 09.564'/W121 52.768'
Height: Lower Lewis River Falls: 43 feet; Middle Lewis River Falls: 33 feet; Upper Lewis River Falls: 58 feet; Taitnapum Falls: 16 feet; Lower Copper Creek Falls: 32 feet; Copper Creek Falls: 26 feet
Difficulty: Easy/Moderate
Approximate hiking time: 2-4 hours
Distance: 7 miles
Trail surface: Hard-packed dirt, duffy, rocky

County: Skamania
Land status: National forest
Trail contact: Gifford Pinchot National Forest, Mt. St. Helens Ranger District, Amboy, WA; www.fs.usda.gov/recarea/giffordpinchot/recarea/?recid=32340; (360) 449-7800
Maps: DeLorme *Washington Atlas & Gazetteer*: Page 88 D4
Northwest Forest Pass or $5 day use fee is required.

Finding the trailhead: From Portland, OR, drive north on I-5 to exit 21 and head east on WA 503 toward Mt. St. Helens for 37 miles. Pass through the town of Cougar, WA, and continue straight as the road turns into FR 90. Proceed for another 18 miles and then at a fork follow FR 90 to the right (south) after the Pine Creek Information Center (really just a kiosk), for another 14.2 miles to the Lower Falls Recreation Area by the "Lower Lewis River Falls" sign. Park at the day-use area (GPS: N46 09.564'/W121 52.768') near the restrooms. The Lower Falls Recreation Area is open May through October and requires a $5 day-use fee or Northwest Forest Pass.

The Hike

Begin by making your way down to the water. There are a number of trails that depart from this area. Some official, some unofficial. Pick one and head down to the water. Once you join the main path paralleling the river, make a right and quickly arrive at Lower Lewis River Falls. There are a couple of viewpoints along this stretch that offer good views of the very photogenic cascade.

Back on the main path, begin hiking upriver. There are a number of paths leading to and from the campground in this area. Stay straight, don't make any lefts, and you'll be fine. Walk over a bridge and a couple of trail junctions before arriving at a bridge crossing over Copper Creek and Lower Copper Creek Falls. Cross the bridge, turn the corner, and immediately arrive at Middle Lewis River Falls. The unique cascade spans the width of the river over a couple of main drops as well as a long, sweeping tumble over bedrock. The best views of the falls can be gained via the beach just prior

Lower Lewis River Falls

Upper Lewis River Falls

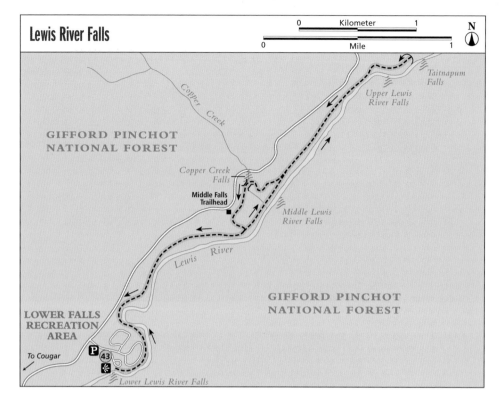

to the falls. Be careful here as slippery rocks and devil's club can make getting a good view difficult and potentially contribute to a painful walk back to the car.

Back at the main trail, the path makes a quick, sharp switchback up to a trail junction. This is the path you will take up to Copper Creek Falls on your return journey, but for now ignore it and head to the right, continuing upriver.

The hike stays straight at this point and after 2.5 total miles of hiking passes a massive Douglas fir tree on the left. Judging by the worn paths leading to the base of the tree, it has entertained a number of visitors. The trail now descends to the river and passes through some very scenic forest before offering the first glimpse of Upper Lewis River Falls. The trail then bends around and crosses a bridge. It then begins a brief but steep ascent to the top of the falls and a series of fenced but occasionally precarious viewpoints.

Continue along the main trail another 0.2 mile to a signed viewpoint of the small but alluring Taitnapum Falls. Turn around here and hike back downriver to the junction above Middle Lewis River Falls. This time, take the side trail to the right and hike a short distance to Copper Creek Falls. The 26-foot cascade jumps off just below a bridge crossing of Copper Creek. The trail now leads up to a parking area just off of FR 90. Take the signed path for the Middle Falls Trail and descend back down to the Lewis River Trail.

Hang a right on the main trail and continue back to the Lower Falls Trailhead.

Miles and Directions

0.0 From the trailhead (GPS: N46 09.564'/W121 52.768'), walk down to the main trail paralleling the Lewis River. Take a right (southwest) and quickly arrive at Lower Lewis River Falls.

0.1 Arrive at Lower Lewis River Falls. Continue upriver (northeast) along the main path.

1.8 Arrive at a bridge crossing Lower Copper Creek Falls. Continue around the corner to Middle Lewis River Falls. From the falls, follow the main trail up a steep switchback and pass a junction leading up to Copper Creek Falls. Stay straight on the main trail.

3.2 Arrive at the Upper Lewis River Falls viewpoints. Continue on the main trail to Taitnapum Falls.

3.4 Arrive at Taitnapum Falls. Head back the way you came.

4.8 At a junction, go right and ascend up to Copper Creek Falls. Continue along the main trail to the trailhead for the Middle Falls. Follow the signed Middle Falls trail down to the main trail.

5.4 At a junction with the Lewis River Trail, go right and follow the main trail back down to the Lower Falls Trailhead.

7.0 Return to the Lower Falls Trailhead.

44 Falls Creek Falls

Truly one of the megastars of Southwest Washington, the list of superlatives that have been used to describe Falls Creek Falls is indeed a long one. It doesn't matter that it's not possible to see all 335 feet of the three-tiered monster at the same time. The size, power, and visual appeal of Falls Creek Falls are something to behold, whether you're gazing at the top tier or the bottom two. Combine the fact that there are a number of good spots from which to sit and take in the falls with the easy-to-digest length of 3.2 total miles and you have a classic dayhike perfect for the family or to show off to out-of-towners.

Start: Lower Falls parking area of FR 3062.
GPS: N43 18.800' / W122 50.117'
Height: 335 feet combined drops
Difficulty: Easy/Moderate
Approximate hiking time: 1.5–3 hours
Distance: 3.2 miles with a 6.3-mile loop option
Trail surface: Hard-packed dirt, duffy, rocky

County: Skamania
Land status: National forest
Trail contact: Gifford Pinchot National Forest, Mt. Adams Ranger District, Trout Lake, WA; www.fs.usda.gov/recarea/giffordpinchot/recarea/?recid=31184; (509) 395-3400
Maps: DeLorme *Washington Atlas & Gazetteer.* Page 100 A5

Finding the trailhead: From Portland, OR, take I-84 east to exit 44 / Cascade Locks. Cross the Bridge of the Gods ($1 toll) and turn right on Highway 14. After 6 miles, turn left to go through Carson. After another 14.5 miles, turn right following a sign for Mt. St. Helens. Almost a mile later, bear right onto gravel FR 3062 and drive 2 miles to its dead end at the Lower Falls parking area (GPS: N43 18.800' / W122 50.117'). There is a seasonal gate closure here from December through March.

The Hike

From the trailhead, the path begins wide and easy through second-growth forest. Stay straight, ignoring a trail to the left after 200 feet. The trail soon arrives at Falls Creek and with the exception of just a couple of cutaways, the path parallels the creek or stays within earshot for the duration of the hike.

After 0.4 mile of hiking, cross over a footbridge that offers a great view of Falls Creek as it squeezes through a narrow gorge. The trail now enters old growth and begins gently rolling, ascending, and descending along the scenic creek. The path occasionally dips in and out of ravines and stays well graded for another 0.5 mile or so.

The path then begins gaining elevation more greedily, pausing briefly at a junction with the upper trail. Save this potential add-on for the way back. The upper trail gives you a heaping helping of extra elevation, but a somewhat tantalizingly disappointing view of Falls Creek Falls' upper tier. For now, stay straight and continue

Falls Creek Falls veils down in its upper section before culminating in a thunderous horsetail into a classic "blue hole" pool.

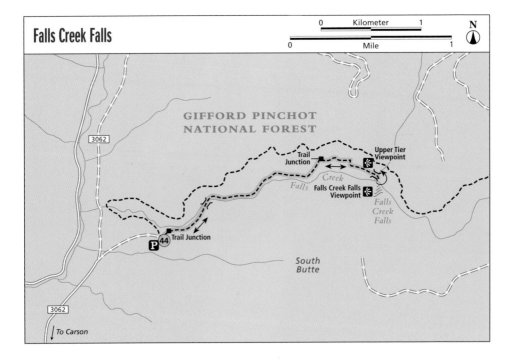

Kilometer

Mile

N

GIFFORD PINCHOT
NATIONAL FOREST

3062

Trail
Junction

Upper Tier
Viewpoint

Creek

Falls   Falls Creek Falls
Viewpoint

Falls
Creek
Falls

Trail Junction

P 44

South
Butte

3062

To Carson

toward the falls. In 0.2 mile more you'll encounter a bridge crossing over a creek that ranges from thundering in spring to bone-dry in late summer. After the bridge, gain one last little chunk of elevation and cross another creek, bridgeless this time. This mini-creek has the potential to moisten your feet in spring, though it's usually a relatively easy rock-hop. This one also dries out pretty well with warmer weather.

After the mini-creek crossing, the trail rounds a bend and the falls will be audible. Look carefully through the trees over the next 100 yards or so as there are a couple of good views of Falls Creek Falls' elusive upper tier, and the top of the second tier. The upper tier will not be visible from where the trail ends near the base of the falls. The trail now loses elevation over the last 500 feet before arriving at Falls Creek Falls.

The view here is of the middle and lower tiers of the cascade, but you won't feel like you're missing anything. They are both graceful and thunderous. Explore the space, have a picnic, and head back the way you came. If you are content with the falls, continue all the way back to the trailhead. If you'd like a little more forest time and a lot more exercise, hang a right at the junction with the upper falls trail marked 152.

Climb a steep 0.2 mile to a T-junction and turn right on the Upper Falls Trail. Hike 0.9 mile more to the Upper Falls viewpoint. As mentioned, it doesn't offer much of a view of the falls, though there are some sketchy scramble paths in the area if you want to attempt to gain a clearer look.

To complete the loop, hike back the way you came and stay straight, remaining on the upper trail when you encounter the junction leading back down to the lower trail. Hike a total of 2.6 miles from the upper falls viewpoint to a junction and turn left, crossing the creek on a footbridge. Turn left after the bridge and upstream along a scenic stretch of Falls Creek for another 0.6 mile to a final junction. Turn right here and arrive at the trailhead a quick 300 feet or so later.

Miles and Directions

0.0 From the trailhead (GPS: N43 18.800'/W122 50.117'), hike to a bridge crossing.

0.4 Cross Falls Creek on a wooden footbridge and continue hiking.

1.2 At a junction (GPS: N43 18.945'/W122 50.162') with the upper falls trail, stay straight and continue hiking.

1.6 Arrive at Falls Creek Falls. Head back the way you came. For the easy out and back, stay straight all the way back to the trailhead after a total of 3.2 miles. The longer loop directions continue below . . .

2.0 At a junction with the upper trail marked #152, turn right and climb steeply.

2.2 At another junction, turn right and continue hiking.

3.1 Arrive at the upper falls viewpoint. Head back the way you came.

4.0 At the junction leading back down to the lower falls, stay straight.

5.7 Turn left at the junction and cross Falls Creek on a footbridge. Turn left after the bridge and continue hiking.

6.3 At the next junction, turn right and continue hiking for ~300 feet back to the trailhead.

6.3 Return to the trailhead.

45 Pothole Falls

If you live even remotely close to the Portland metro area and you haven't paid Lacamas Park in nearby Camas, WA, a visit, this is a situation you should remedy. The park has all of the family-friendly trappings you would expect: barbecue/picnic areas, a playground, and more. But it's also home to Round Lake and the Lacamas River. The hiking paths within the park visit exquisite wildflower meadows, impressive swatches of old-growth forest, popular swimming holes, and a handful of waterfalls—including what is believed to be the only non-basalt waterfall in the Columbia River Gorge.

Start: Lacamas Park parking lot off NE Everett Street in Camas, WA. GPS: N45 36.236'/W122 24.425'
Height: Pothole Falls: 20 feet; Lower Falls: 30 feet; Woodburn Falls: 20 feet
Difficulty: Easy
Approximate hiking time: 1.5-3 hours
Distance: 3.2 miles

Trail surface: Hard-packed dirt, duffy, rocky
County: Clark
Land status: County park
Trail contact: Clark County Parks, Vancouver, WA; www.clark.wa.gov/publicworks/parks; (360) 397-2285
Maps: DeLorme *Washington Atlas & Gazetteer*: Page 99 D10

Finding the trailhead: From Vancouver, head east on WA 14 to exit 12 in Camas. Stay on 6th Avenue going straight until you reach Garfield. Turn left on Garfield. Follow the WA 500 signs up the hill veering left just before the high school and right at the stop sign where the highway meets Everett. Follow Everett for about a mile to a parking lot (GPS: N45 36.236'/W122 24.425') on the right just past the light for Lake Road. Keep a sharp eye here, as it's easy to miss. If you get to 35th Avenue, you've gone too far.

The Hike

From the parking area (GPS: N45 36.236'/W122 24.425'), follow the paved path into the main park area and make your way toward Round Lake. Once you've made it to the path that parallels the lake, make a right and continue hiking. The trail passes over a dam at the base of the lake and splinters into numerous paths. Stay to the right as much as possible here, staying close to Lacamas Creek. After a half mile of total hiking, you will reach Pothole Falls.

A very popular swimming hole in summer, Pothole Falls is unique in appearance as well as composition. Water fills and swirls in small pothole-shaped pools in the bedrock giving the falls a wide range of foot-dipping options and flow patterns, depending on water levels. Continue hiking downstream. The path reaches some rocky outcroppings that afford the last view of the falls before turning a corner and descending steeply into attractive woods populated by western red cedar. Stay straight at a junction and follow the path as it circles around and returns to the creek.

The namesake potholes near Pothole Falls

The next section of trail is extremely attractive in autumn as big-leaf maples line the trail with color. After 1.1 miles of total hiking arrive at a bridge crossing the creek and the Lower Falls. Walk out onto the bridge for views of the creek and the Lower Falls, but don't cross it. Some good views of the falls can also be had via some boot paths just downstream from the bridge.

Make a left at the bridge, following a wide gravel path. Pass a junction only 30 feet or so beyond the bridge and make a left at the second junction that appears shortly after the first. The path now ascends into the woods. After 0.2 mile stay right to remain on the main trail and hike to a T-junction with a gravel road. Go left here and follow the road for 0.4 mile to an easy-to-miss junction on the left side of the gravel road. Take this path down into the woods. Ignore a junction and continue on the main path, eventually bending to the left and arriving at Woodburn Falls.

Nobody is going to confuse Woodburn Falls with the mighty Multnomah Falls, but the 20-foot cascade possesses its own low-flow beauty. Backtrack up to the gravel road and make a left. At the next junction make a right, heading uphill, and about 300 feet later make a left at another junction, heading downhill, soon arriving back at Round Lake. Follow the path along the lake, eventually reaching the dam. Continue hiking back to the trailhead.

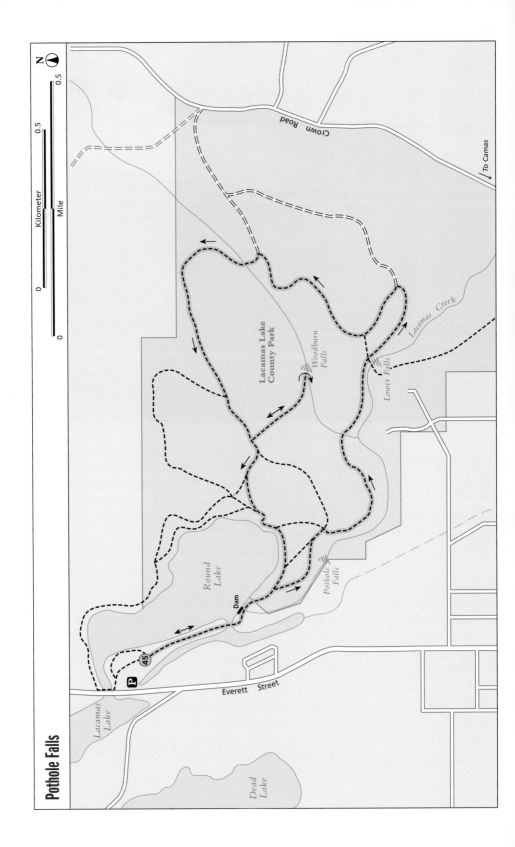

Pothole Falls

Miles and Directions

0.0 From the trailhead (GPS: N45 36.236' / W122 24.425') take the main paved path to the right, following the lake. Cross the dam.

0.3 Arrive at a junction on the other side of the dam. Take the path to the right, staying close to the creek.

0.4 At the next junction, stay right, following the creek.

0.5 Check out the Potholes, then continue hiking.

0.8 Stay straight (slight right) at a junction, continuing on the main path.

1.1 Cross a footbridge over the top of Lower Falls, then turn left, immediately passing one junction before arriving at a second.

1.2 Make a left at an Access Road junction.

1.6 At a T-junction with a gravel road, turn left.

2.0 Look for an easy-to-miss junction on the left, and take this path to its end at Woodburn Falls, passing a junction leading left along the way. Backtrack to the gravel road and turn left.

2.6 At this junction, make a left heading up hill.

2.7 At another junction, turn left, switch-backing down to Round Lake.

2.8 Down by the lake, go right, staying close to the lake and arriving back at the dam. Cross the dam and hike back to the trailhead.

3.2 Return to the trailhead.

46 Hardy Falls/Rodney Falls

Contrary to popular belief, there are waterfalls on the Washington side of the Columbia River Gorge. While throngs of tourists try to out-latte each other at Multnomah Falls, Hardy and Rodney Falls sit in relative obscurity on the other side of the river. Beacon Rock State Park is home to more than the volcanic monolith that guards the banks of the Columbia. It's also where the short hike to Hardy and Rodney Falls begins. If you're up to the task, you can continue past the falls and complete a classic loop hike that visits the summit of Hamilton Mountain.

Start: Marked trailhead off parking lot on campground access road in Beacon Rock State Park. GPS: N45 37.958'/W122 01.192'
Height: Hardy Falls: 90 feet; Rodney Falls: 80 feet
Difficulty: Easy/Difficult (depending on route choice)
Approximate hiking time: 1–2 hours
Distance: 2.2 miles out and back to the falls or 7.6-mile loop summit of Hamilton Mountain

Trail surface: Hard-packed dirt, duffy, rocky
County: Skamania
Land status: State park
Trail contact: Washington State Parks, Beacon Rock State Park, Skamania, WA; www.parks.wa.gov/474/Beacon-Rock; (509) 427-8265
Maps: DeLorme *Washington Atlas & Gazetteer*: Page 100 C3

Finding the trailhead: From Vancouver, take WA 14 east for 34 miles to Beacon Rock. Carefully bear left crossing oncoming traffic onto the campground access road. Drive 0.3 mile to the marked trailhead (GPS: N45 37.958'/W122 01.192') off the parking lot on the right. (Discovery Pass or $10 day-use fee is required.)

The Hike

Start from the trailhead next to a playground and a set of bathrooms. The trail begins an immediate and steady ascent through second-growth forest before passing beneath a set of power lines at the 0.4-mile mark. At a half mile ignore a junction on the left leading to a campground.

Continue the steady climb, crossing over a footbridge and arriving at a junction leading down to the viewpoint of Hardy Falls after just under a mile of total hiking. The first viewing area offers a decent but obscured look at the top of Hardy Falls. A steep path continues down farther and, while it technically gets you closer to the falls, the view doesn't get any better without a dangerous scramble. Head back up to the main trail and turn right, continuing a short distance to Rodney Falls and another junction.

Turn left and walk up to the Pool of Winds viewpoint. Rodney Falls' first drop spills into a rock-guarded nook, forming a deep pool of water that also produces

The view from the footbridge at the base of wild and woolly Rodney Falls.

Hardy Falls/Rodney Falls

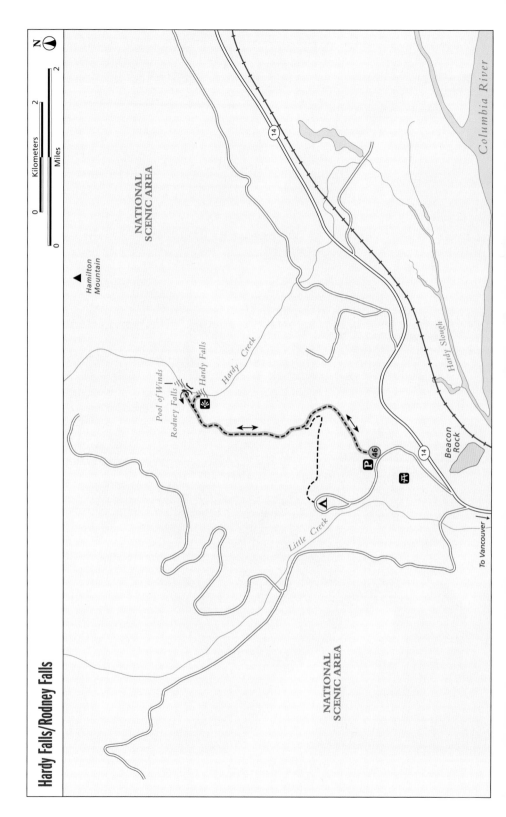

a good amount of wind and spray. During periods of high water it can be almost impossible to get a good look or a photo without getting a shower. Walk back down to the previous junction and follow the path down to a bridge that crosses over Hardy Creek near the base of Rodney Falls. From the bridge, backtrack the way you came down to the trailhead.

Alternately, if you're up for more exercise and some stunning gorge views, continue across the bridge and hike 0.2 mile to another junction. Stay right and begin the steady, vista-laden climb to the summit of Hamilton Mountain. At a T-junction near the summit, turn left and follow the trail as it makes its way to a saddle with great views of the gorge, Table Mountain, and Mt. Adams.

Continue hiking to a junction with a gravel road and turn left, descending 1 mile to another junction. Turn left and enjoy another mellow, 1-mile descent to yet another junction. Turn right here and continue back down to the trailhead.

Miles and Directions

0.0 From the trailhead (GPS: N45 37.958' / W122 01.192') hike to a junction with the Hardy Falls viewpoint. Ignore a junction to the left beneath a set of power lines at the .5 mile mark.

0.9 At a junction, turn right for the Hardy Falls viewpoint. Walk down to an obscured view of Hardy Falls and then walk back to the main trail and take a right.

1.1 At the next junction, go left on a side trail that ends at the Pool of Winds and the first drop of Rodney Falls. Walk back down to the previous junction and continue on the main trail down to a bridge that crosses Hardy Creek at the base of Rodney Falls. Head back the way you came.

2.2 Return to the trailhead.

To continue the Hamilton Mountain loop, cross the bridge and continue hiking.

1.4 At a junction, bear right and continue hiking.

3.2 At a T-junction, go left, hiking along a ridge and a saddle area at the back of Hamilton Mountain.

4.1 At a junction with a gravel road, head left, downhill.

5.1 Turn left at the next junction and continue hiking.

6.2 Turn right at the following junction, heading back down to the trailhead.

7.6 Return to the trailhead.

47 Loowit Falls

Mt. St. Helens' Crater Glacier is both the youngest and fastest growing glacier in the United States. It is also responsible for the 186-foot Loowit Falls that tumbles into Loowit Canyon less than a mile from the toe of the glacier. The hike to Loowit Falls is remarkable for several reasons, not the least of which being the opportunity to observe and experience firsthand the rapid recovery of flora and fauna in the blast zone nearly 35 years after the eruption.

Start: Pick up the marked Truman Trail at the south end of the Windy Ridge parking lot. GPS: N46 14.931'/W122 08.168'
Height: 186 feet
Difficulty: Moderate
Approximate hiking time: 3–5 hours
Distance: 8.8 miles
Trail surface: Rocky, dusty

County: Skamania
Land status: National forest
Trail contact: Mt. St. Helens National Volcanic Monument; www.fs.usda.gov/mountsthelens; (360) 449-7800
Maps: DeLorme *Washington Atlas & Gazetteer.* Page 88 C2

Finding the trailhead: From Portland, take I-5 north to exit 21. Turn right and drive 88 miles, passing through the town of Cougar. Along the way WA 503 will become FR 90. At the Pine Creek Information Station stay straight onto FR 25 for 25 miles. Turn left onto FR 99 and drive 16 miles to the road's end (GPS: N46 14.931'/W122 08.168') at the Windy Ridge Viewpoint. (Northwest Forest Pass or $5 day-use fee is required.)

The Hike

The hike begins at the south end of the parking area on the Truman Trail. Follow this gravel road for 2 miles to the road's end, passing a junction with the Abraham Trail at the 1.7-mile mark along the way. Continue straight onto the Windy Trail.

At the 2.8-mile mark, reach another junction and turn right onto the Loowit Trail, following signs for Loowit Falls. On a clear day the trail offers stunning views of Mt. Adams and, as the hike progresses, wide-open views of Spirit Lake and Mt. Rainier in the distance.

Continue hiking as the trail winds its way closer to the crater, in and out of ravines along a lunar landscape that supports a variety of wildflowers. At 3.2 miles the trail crosses paths with a spring and a verdant oasis where you stand a good chance of getting wet feet.

As the hike continues and the landscape views continue to broaden, you'll reach a signed junction with the side trail leading to Loowit Falls at 3.8 miles. Turn left onto the spur trail and climb steeply for half a mile to the viewpoint of Loowit Falls. Being such a relatively new geological feature, and in an area where change is happening at

Loowit Falls' double horsetail powers through the "blast zone" with Mt. St. Helens looming in the distance.

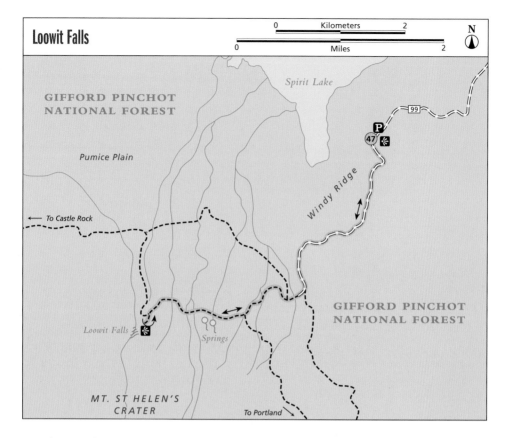

Loowit Falls

GIFFORD PINCHOT
NATIONAL FOREST

Spirit Lake

Pumice Plain

Windy Ridge

← To Castle Rock

GIFFORD PINCHOT
NATIONAL FOREST

Loowit Falls

Springs

MT. ST HELEN'S
CRATER

To Portland

such a rapid rate, the falls are morphing from month to month. Take it all in, but also step cautiously in this area. Head back the way you came.

Miles and Directions

0.0 From the trailhead (GPS: N46 14.931' / W122 08.168') hike 2 miles along the Truman Trail, a gravel road, to its end.

2.0 At the end of the gravel road, continue straight onto the Windy Trail.

2.8 At a junction, take a right onto the Loowit Trail.

3.8 Take a left at a junction with the spur trail leading to Loowit Falls.

4.4 Arrive at the Loowit Falls viewpoint. Head back the way you came.

8.8 Return to the trailhead and parking area.

48 Last Hope Falls

It does require a bit of a drive, that's for sure. But this is a fairly unusual cascade. Last Hope Falls, named after the old Last Hope Mine, separates, slides, and plunges in a number of different formations depending on the flow, which varies considerably depending on the season. Located just within the blast zone from the 1980 Mt. St. Helens eruption, Last Hope Falls is surrounded by lush plant growth, all of which has recolonized the area within the last 30 years.

Start: Signed trailhead off FR 2162. GPS: N46 21.011'/W122 06.580'
Height: 38 feet
Difficulty: Easy
Approximate hiking time: 30–60 minutes
Distance: 0.6 mile out-and-back
Trail surface: Hard-packed dirt, duffy, rocky

County: Skamania
Land status: National forest
Trail contact: Mt. St. Helens National Volcanic Monument; www.fs.usda.gov/mountsthelens; (360) 449-7800
Maps: DeLorme *Washington Atlas & Gazetteer:* Page 88 B3

Finding the trailhead: From Randle, take FR 25 south a short ways and bear right onto FR 26 just after crossing the Cispus River. After a little over 12 miles of driving, turn right onto FR 2162, following signs for the Green River Trail. Just before 2.5 miles of gravel-road driving, stay left at a fork and look for an easy-to-miss, signed trail on the right (GPS: N46 21.011'/W122 06.580').

The Hike

Follow the trail on the north side of the gravel road into the woods. The forest here is primarily regrowth some 35 years old, as the area was in the blast zone when Mt. St. Helens erupted in 1980. In summer, huckleberries and thimbleberries line the path for the entire 0.3 mile it takes to reach a viewpoint with a bench to soak in the forest scene.

The word "viewpoint" might be stretching things a tad because a good portion of the falls is obscured by alder trees and other overzealous native greenery sprouted up since 1980. Scramble around to find your own best views of the falls, but exercise caution as the penalty for making a mistake would be pretty stiff. When you've found your best view, enjoy it for a few minutes, snap some pictures, and then turn around and retrace your steps back to the trailhead.

Last Hope Falls

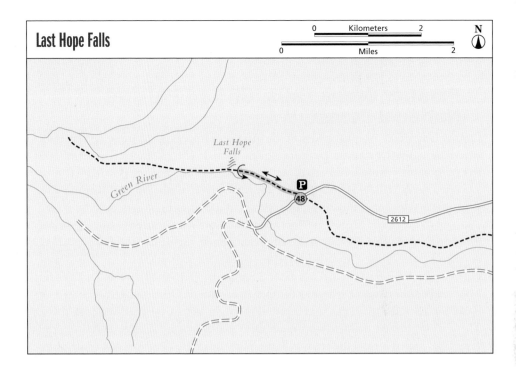

Miles and Directions

0.0 From the trailhead (GPS: N46 21.011'/W122 06.580'), hike 0.3 mile to a bench and a view of Last Hope Falls.

0.3 Arrive at the Last Hope Falls viewpoint. Head back the way you came.

0.6 Return to the trailhead.

Honorable Mentions

T. Panther Creek Falls, Gifford Pinchot National Forest, WA

Panther Creek Falls is arguably one of the most jaw-droppingly picturesque waterfalls anywhere in the Northwest. Imagine a giant natural spring consisting of about 100 feet or so of intertwining ribbons of water and moss, gently flowing down the face of a massive basalt wall. Now also picture a pristine creek rushing toward that palisade, with a small segment of the stream splintering off just prior to impact, creating a delicate, veil-like cascade. Meanwhile the majority of the creek careens into the spring, becoming a turbulent 70-foot waterfall. Once united, the waters travel a very short distance before falling over a lower 30-foot tier. This is Panther Creek Falls. From Carson, take Wind River Road north for 5.8 miles to Old State Road and turn right. Then make an immediate left onto Panther Creek Road. Drive along Panther Creek Road for 7.4 miles to a large gravel pit on the right side of the road and park there. There is no marked trailhead and there may or may not be signage indicating the waterfall. Cross the road and start walking south, or in the direction you came from, for about 150 feet to the easy-to-miss trail on the side of the road. The path descends

A hiker breathes in some negative ions at Panther Creek Falls.

quickly and leads to a large viewing platform roughly 150 yards from the trailhead. There is a scramble path about 75 feet to the left (south) side of the viewing platform that leads down to the base of the falls. It is, however, a very steep and dangerous path made all the more so in wet conditions. It requires a couple of rock-climbing maneuvers and a certain level of off-trail experience. GPS: N45 52.036' / W121 49.718'

U. Lower Rock Creek Falls, Stevenson, WA

Located in the area of the landslide that gave birth to the native "Bridge of the Gods" legend, this 53-foot cascade is tangible, visible evidence of the geology of the Columbia River Gorge and its ever-eroding ways. The canyon carved out by Rock Creek

Lower Rock Creek Falls

shows a number of exposed layers of earth including conglomerate bedrock and volcanic ash. It is also unstable and susceptible to mini-slides. The creek is capable of a rather heavy flow during high water season, adding to the instability. From Vancouver, WA, drive east for ~40 miles on WA 14 and take a left (north) onto Rock Creek Drive (also signed for "Skamania Lodge"), and follow it for 0.75 miles and then turn left onto Ryan Allen Road. Make a quick right and follow 1 Man Cemetery Road for about 0.75 mile before turning right onto First Falls View Road, which soon dead-ends. Park where you can, but avoid private property. Hop over a wooden barrier and take a very steep boot path about 300 feet down to the creek and Lower Rock Creek Falls (GPS: N45 41.951'/W121 53.762'). There are a couple of different viewpoints of the falls in this area, but exercise extreme caution as the area is unstable.

V. Heaven and Hell Falls/Steep Creek Falls, Stevenson, WA

This pair of drive-up falls is less than half a mile away from each other and could (perhaps should) be visited in the same go. Summer wandering around both of the falls

Steep Creek Falls

can lead to some choice swimming holes. The 52-foot Steep Creek Falls is particularly photogenic during both full and low flow; in addition, it affords the possibility of walking behind the falls when water levels are low enough. Heaven and Hell Falls is a 26-foot, segmented horsetail cascade that can be difficult to get a good view of, but the area above the falls is where the best swimming is located. From Vancouver, WA, drive east for ~40 miles on WA 14 and take a left (north) onto Rock Creek Drive (also signed for "Skamania Lodge"), follow it for 0.75 mile, and then turn left onto Ryan Allen Road. Drive 1 mile and take a left onto Red Bluff Road, which turns into Rock Creek Road. After 2.5 miles of gravel-road driving, stay left at a fork and continue another 3 miles to a bridge crossing of Rock Creek. Steep Creek Falls is on the left. Walk or drive a short 0.3 mile up the road beyond Steep Creek Falls and look for a boot path descending down to the creek on the left. There is a small campsite at the top of Heaven & Hell Falls. The falls themselves are tough to get a good look at depending on water levels, but downstream scramblers will be rewarded for their efforts with the best possible view. GPS: N45 44.884' / W121 58.952'

W. Sunset Falls, Gifford Pinchot National Forest, WA

A nice little out-of-the-way 14-foot falls. Sunset Falls splits off into a handful of separate channels depending on the season, making it a good photo study. It's debatable whether Sunset Falls is the type of cascade that warrants its own trip, especially if you're driving a considerable distance. But if you happen to be camping at the Sunset Falls Campground or on your way to do some hiking around Silver Star Mountain,

Sunset Falls

it's certainly worth a stop. From Battle Ground, WA, drive east on Lucia Falls Road for 5.8 miles and then turn right onto Sunset Falls Road. Drive 7.5 more miles to the signed day-use parking area and follow a short path to the falls (GPS: N45 49.058'/W122 14.973').

X. Iron Creek Falls, Gifford Pinchot National Forest, WA

Located just off of FR 25 near Mt. St. Helens, Iron Creek Falls is attractive enough to warrant its own day trip. But because it's a drive-up, you could easily tack a visit to these falls onto any number of Mt. St. Helens area–based outings. The 40-foot, multi-pronged cascade plunges into an inviting albeit chilly splash pool exquisitely framed by verdant Northwest forest. The areas at the base of the falls—including behind the falls, and downstream from the falls—are worth exploring and certainly photogenic, so make sure to spend some quality time there. From the trailhead the path descends quickly to a viewpoint of the falls a short 500 feet from where you started. If you brought water shoes or you don't mind wet feet, continue down to the creek and explore at will. From Randle, WA, drive south on FR 25 south for 19 miles to the signed Iron Creek Falls trailhead and parking area on the left. Follow the path 500 feet to the falls. GPS: N46 19.840'/W121 58.239'

Iron Creek Falls

Y. Lava Canyon Falls, Mt. St. Helens National Volcanic Monument, WA

This 5-mile out-and-back hike takes you through an otherworldly canyon formed by lava flows two millennia ago and then scoured clean (again) by mudflows following the big 1980 eruption of nearby Mt. St. Helens. The first half mile of the hike is paved and handicapped-accessible, and features interpretive displays full of information on volcanism and how lava carved out the gorge below. From there the trail turns to dirt and descends quickly into the gorge—watch your step! Highlights of the hike include traversing a bouncy suspension footbridge over the Muddy River and then viewing Lava Canyon Falls, which run 132 feet down a steep basalt chute before hurtling downstream. Other nearby attractions on the south side of Mt. St. Helens include Ape Cave (GPS: N46 06.519' / W122 12.623'), a lava tube running for more than 13,000 feet under the surface of an ancient lava flow that visitors can explore with headlamps, and the Trail of Two Forests (GPS: N46 05.940' / W122 12.726'), where a crusty ancient lava flow overtook a forest and solidified before the trees could burn up, leaving gaping holes in the still intact and hardened lava bed. From Woodland, WA, drive east on WA 503, which becomes FR 90, for 35 miles, then turn left (north) onto FR 83 and follow it east for 11 miles to its terminus at the Lava Canyon parking lot. GPS: N46 10.705' / W122 03.155'

A hiker crosses the suspension bridge over the Muddy River en route to the Lava Canyon Falls on the south side of Mt. St. Helens National Volcanic Monument.

The Art of Hiking

GETTING INTO SHAPE

Unless you want to be sore—and possibly have to shorten your trip or vacation—be sure to get in shape before a big hike. If you're terribly out of shape, start a walking program early, preferably eight weeks in advance. Start with a fifteen-minute walk during your lunch hour or after work and gradually increase your walking time to an hour. You should also increase your elevation gain. Walking briskly up hills really strengthens your leg muscles and gets your heart rate up. If you work in a storied office building, take the stairs instead of the elevator. If you prefer going to a gym, walk the treadmill or use a stair machine. You can further increase your strength and endurance by walking with a loaded backpack. Stationary exercises you might consider are squats, leg lifts, sit-ups, and push-ups. Other good ways to get in shape include biking, running, aerobics, and, of course, short hikes. Stretching before and after a hike keeps muscles flexible and helps avoid injuries.

TRAIL ETIQUETTE

Leave no trace. Always leave an area just like you found it—if not better than you found it. Avoid camping in fragile, alpine meadows and along the banks of streams and lakes. Use a camp stove versus building a wood fire. Pack up all of your trash and extra food. Bury human waste at least 100 feet from water sources under 6 to 8 inches of topsoil. Don't bathe with soap in a lake or stream—use prepackaged moistened towels to wipe off sweat and dirt, or bathe in the water without soap.

Stay on the trail. It's true, a path anywhere leads nowhere new, but paths serve an important purpose: They limit impact on natural areas. Straying from a designated trail may seem innocent, but it can cause damage to sensitive areas—damage that may take years to recover, if it can recover at all. Even simple shortcuts can be destructive. So, please, stay on the trail.

WATER

Even in frigid conditions, you need at least two quarts of water a day to function efficiently. Add heat and taxing terrain and you can bump that figure up to one gallon. That's simply a base to work from—your metabolism and your level of conditioning can raise or lower that amount. Unless you know your level, assume that you need one gallon of water a day. Now, where do you plan on getting the water?

The easiest solution is to bring water with you. Natural water sources can be loaded with intestinal disturbers, such as bacteria, viruses, and fertilizers. *Giardia lamblia*, the most common of these disturbers, is a protozoan parasite that lives part of its life cycle as a cyst in water sources. The parasite spreads when mammals defecate in water sources. Once ingested, *Giardia* can induce cramping, diarrhea, vomiting, and fatigue within two days to two weeks after ingestion. If you believe you've contracted giardiasis, see a doctor immediately, as it is treatable with prescription drugs. If you're hiking too far to bring all the water you'll need, carry a lightweight water filter so you can get water from streams and lakes.

DEHYDRATION

Have you ever hiked in hot weather and had a roaring headache and felt fatigued after only a few miles? More than likely you were dehydrated. Symptoms of dehydration include fatigue, headache, and decreased coordination and judgment. When you are hiking, your body's rate of fluid loss depends on the outside temperature, humidity, altitude, and your activity level. On average, a hiker walking in warm weather will lose four liters of fluid a day. That fluid loss is easily replaced by normal consumption of liquids and food. However, if a hiker is walking briskly in hot, dry weather and hauling a heavy pack, he or she can lose one to three liters of water an hour. It's important to always carry plenty of water and to stop often and drink fluids regularly, even if you aren't thirsty.

HIKING WITH YOUR DOG

Bringing your furry friend with you is always more fun than leaving him behind. Our canine pals make great trail buddies because they never complain and always make good company.

Before you plan outdoor adventures with your dog, make sure he's in shape for the trail. Take him on your daily runs or walks. Also, be sure he has a firm grasp of the basics of canine etiquette and behavior, and that he can sit, lie down, stay, and come on command. Purchase collapsible water and dog food bowls for your dog. If you are hiking on rocky terrain or in the snow, you can purchase footwear for your dog that will protect his feet from cuts and bruises.

Once on the trail, keep your dog under control. You can buy a flexi-lead that allows your dog to go exploring along the trail, while allowing you the ability to reel him in should another hiker approach or should he decide to chase a rabbit. Always obey leash laws and be sure to bury your dog's waste or pack it in resealable plastic bags.

HIKING WITH CHILDREN

Hiking with children is all about seeing and experiencing nature through their eyes. Kids like to explore and have fun. They like to stop and point out bugs and plants, look under rocks, jump in puddles, and throw sticks. If you're taking a toddler or young child on a hike, start with a trail that you're familiar with. Trails that have interesting things for kids, like piles of leaves to play in or a small stream to wade through during the summer, will make the hike much more enjoyable for them and will keep them from getting bored.

You can keep your child's attention if you have a strategy before starting on the trail. Using games is not only an effective way to keep a child's attention, it's also a great way to teach him or her about nature. Quiz children on the names of plants and animals. If your children are old enough, let them carry their own daypacks filled with treats and a favorite (small) toy. So that you are sure to go at their pace and not yours, let them lead the way. Playing follow the leader works particularly well when you have a group of children. Have each child take a turn at being the leader.

TICKS

Ticks can carry diseases such as Rocky Mountain spotted fever and Lyme disease. The best defense is, of course, prevention. If you know you're going to be hiking through an area littered with ticks, wear long pants and a long sleeved shirt. You can apply a permethrin repellent to your clothing and a Deet repellent to exposed skin. At the end of your hike, do a spot check for ticks (and insects in general). If you do find a tick embedded in your skin, grab the body of the tick firmly between two fingers and gently pull it away from the skin with a twisting motion, making sure to pull out the head. Clean the affected area with an antibacterial cleanser and then apply triple antibiotic ointment. Monitor the area for a few days. If irritation persists or a white spot develops, see a doctor for possible infection.

POISON IVY, OAK, AND SUMAC

These skin irritants can be found most anywhere in North America and come in the form of a bush or a vine, having leaflets in groups of three, five, seven, or nine. Learn how to spot the plants. The oil they secrete can cause an allergic reaction in the form of blisters, usually about twelve hours after exposure. The itchy rash can last from ten days to several weeks. The best defense against these irritants is to wear clothing that covers the arms, legs, and torso. There are also nonprescription lotions you can apply to exposed skin that guard against the effects of poison ivy/oak/sumac and can be washed off with soap and water.

If you think you were in contact with the plants, after hiking (or even on the trail during longer hikes) wash with soap and water. Taking a hot shower with soap after you return home will also help to remove any lingering oil from your skin.

Should you contract a rash from any of these plants, use an antihistamine to reduce the itching and apply a topical lotion to dry up the area. If the rash spreads, consult your doctor.

LIGHTNING

Thunderstorms build over the mountains almost every day during the summer. Lightning is generated by thunderheads and can strike without warning, even several miles away from the nearest overhead cloud. The best rule of thumb is to start leaving exposed peaks, ridges, and canyon rims by about noon. This time can vary a little depending on storm buildup. Keep an eye on cloud formation and don't underestimate how fast a storm can build. The bigger they get, the more likely a thunderstorm will happen. Lightning takes the path of least resistance, so if you're the high point, it might choose you. Ducking under a rock overhang is dangerous as you form the shortest path between the rock and ground. If you dash below treeline, avoid standing under the only or the tallest tree. If you are caught above treeline, stay away from anything metal you might be carrying. Move down off the ridge slightly to a low, treeless point and squat until the storm passes. If you have an insulating pad, squat on it. Avoid having both your hands and feet touching the ground at once and never lay flat. If you hear a buzzing sound or feel your hair standing on end, move quickly as an electrical charge is building up.

HUNTING SEASON

Hunting is a popular sport in the United States, especially during rifle season in October and November. Hiking is still enjoyable in those months in many areas, but take a few precautions. First, learn when the different hunting seasons start and end in the area in which you'll be hiking. During this time frame, be sure to wear at least a blaze orange hat, and possibly put an orange vest over your pack. Don't be surprised to see hunters in camo outfits carrying bows or rifles around during their season. If you would feel more comfortable without hunters around, hike in national parks and monuments or state and local parks where hunting is not allowed.

Photo Credits

All photos copyright © Roddy Scheer, www.roddyscheer.com, except as noted below:

Adam Sawyer: Chinook Falls, Covell Creek Falls, Falls Creek Falls, Loowit Falls, Lower Lewis River Falls, Lower Rock Creek Falls, Panther Creek Falls, Pothole Falls, Siouxon Falls, Steep Creek Falls, Upper Lewis River Falls, Wildcat Falls

Jason Keene: Last Hope Falls

Melinda Muckenthaler and Timothy Burke: Sunset Falls, Hardy Falls

Brad Bailey: Angel Falls

Jamie Chabot: Rodney Falls

Visit Spokane: Liberty Lake Falls

Hike Index

Mt. Rainier and Vicinity

Southwest Washington

About the Authors

Roddy Scheer is a writer and photographer specializing in nature, the outdoors, environmental issues, and travel. He has been living in and exploring the Pacific Northwest since 1999 and has become a trusted source for information on the region's outdoor recreation opportunities. His writing has appeared regularly in publications including *Seattle* magazine, *Northwest Travel* and *E/The Environmental Magazine*, and he has coauthored the books *Mt. St. Helens: The Continuing Story* (KC Publications, 2005) and *Earthtalk: Questions & Answers About Our Environment* (Plume, 2009). Meanwhile, his stock photography collection of iconic Northwest nature and wildlife subjects includes more than 10,000 images and is represented by the Danita Delimont Agency, while his fine art prints have been featured in three solo exhibitions and are for sale directly via his website and through a handful of galleries. For more information, check out roddyscheer.com.

Adam Sawyer is an outdoor and travel writer and photographer based out of Portland, Oregon. His work has appeared in *Northwest Travel*, *Portland Monthly*, *Columbia River Gorge*, *Central Oregon*, and *Backpacker* magazines. He currently pens articles as the Portland Hiking Examiner for Examiner.com and authored the biweekly column "Portland Family Outdoors" for Craigmore Creations. He was the cohost of the KEEN HybridLife Radio Show for its duration and now serves as a brand ambassador for the company. He is also the author of *Hiking Waterfalls in Oregon* (FalconGuides).

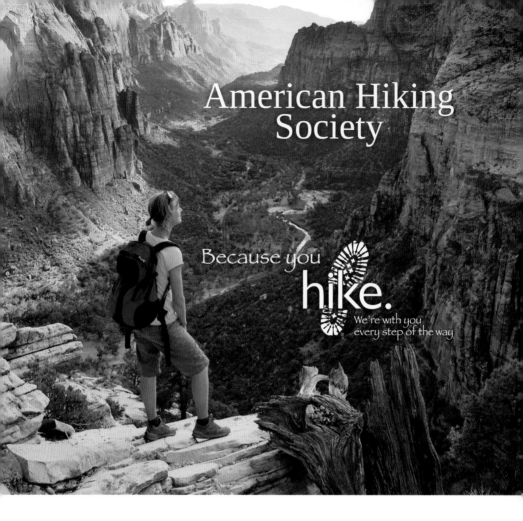

American Hiking Society

Because you hike.

We're with you every step of the way

As a national voice for hikers, **American Hiking Society** works every day:

- Building and maintaining hiking trails
- Educating and supporting hikers by providing information and resources
- Supporting hiking and trail organizations nationwide
- Speaking for hikers in the halls of Congress and with federal land managers

Whether you're a casual hiker or a seasoned backpacker, become a member of American Hiking Society and join the national hiking community! You'll enjoy great member benefits and help preserve the nation's hiking trails, so tomorrow's hike is even better than today's. We invite you to join us now!

American Hiking Society

www.AmericanHiking.org • info@AmericanHiking.org